# Transformed
## *A fresh look at Romans 12*

By
Robert Stagmer

INFINITY
PUBLISHING

Bible quotations are from the King James Bible unless otherwise noted.

Copyright © 2011 by Robert Stagmer

ISBN 0-7414-6842-5

Printed in the United States of America

Published September 2011

INFINITY PUBLISHING
1094 New DeHaven Street, Suite 100
West Conshohocken, PA 19428-2713
Toll-free (877) BUY BOOK
Local Phone (610) 941-9999
Fax (610) 941-9959
Info@buybooksontheweb.com
www.buybooksontheweb.com

# ACKNOWLEDGEMENTS

Annette Stagmer for tireless rewriting, encouragement, editing, and support

Donna Jarboe for a final edit and suggestions.

Dave Severary for an extensive read through and suggestions

Barbara and Randy Walter for excellent suggestions

Michele Perrera and Kathy Black for technical support and encouragement

The congregation of the former The Spirit and the Bride Church especially Ed and Sharon Thomas

And our dearest friend and fellow minister, Iris Owens (deceased)

# CONTENTS

*Robert explaining the
Mystery of the Shofar
at Shavout service*

# PREFACE

It has been said that God has no PLAN B. God has only one plan. He has a specific plan for a person's life. Fortunately, God has plans even for people who fail. (That's all of us.) As sinners, we fail to conform to God's design for His creation. God's grace enables him to wipe away the record of failure. He is ready to stamp your life's performance "ACCEPTED."

That is God's love. He desires to make us whole. It is His personal acceptance of us that enables us to grow.

**Genesis 1:28** tells us that after making man in His image, "...God blessed them, and God said unto them, "Be fruitful and multiply, and replenish the earth, and subdue it and have dominion..." This verse reveals the fivefold purpose of creation for all of us. The purpose of this book is to help you discover your place in God's unfolding plan of creation.

Every minute of every day you are faced with choices. The Christian's challenge is to face those choices with a godly character. Even when we refuse to make a choice, we have chosen. As ambassadors of the Lord Jesus Christ, we are not called to be reactors to circumstances. We are not to allow the external influences of the world to shape and guide our lives. Rather, we are to be responsible for being the stewards who create. We take an active role by planning to allow God, through His Spirit and His Word to conform us to His image.

Either you passively react to circumstances allowing the externals of the world to shape you, or you become active by participating in the things of God and being shaped by them. The basic choice we face, and the continuous choice we face is whether to become active or to remain passive. Christians are activators by nature. We are responsible for initiating a course of action, through God's creative power and His Word, rather than letting circumstances dictate our course to us.

# CHAPTER ONE

# Making Worship Your First Priority

## GRADUATION

I'm not complaining, but… You see, things might have been different. If I'd gotten the grades in high School; if my father hadn't been ill and died when I was eighteen; if the business had been sold….

After high school, I worked for six months in my dad's drug store, but the business, which had existed for thirty-five years as an extension of my father's and grandfather's personalities and personal good will, was failing with dad's deteriorating health. In order to bring more money into the family household I started to work at the B. & O. Railroad central office, in Baltimore city. I took a night shift job so that I could take shorthand and typing courses. Shortly thereafter my father passed away and the business was seized by creditors and sold at auction. All the family ended up with was a few mementos.

I really didn't like the secretarial course and I wasn't very good at it, so I quit. My night shift job was running I.B.M. unit record machines (the ancestors of computers). So I went looking for a job as a data processing operator.

It turned out that I had been trained, robot-like, to perform a few simple tasks and knew nothing about the complexities of the machinery and their procedures.

It was the first time in my life that I experienced such a challenge. By the end of the first week I had learned more than the bosses thought possible; by the end of the second week my job was secure. I saw a whole new set of possibilities for my life.

My boss began encouraging me to go to night school and take accounting courses. My older brother had just passed the C.P.A. exam so I followed in his footsteps. Now I had a new priority. After four years of working and paying my own way, I graduated, with honors and I passed the C.P.A. test.

It was a relief to be finished the program, but I missed the challenge of school. I changed jobs several times in the next few years. I realized that the certificate in Accounting wasn't enough. I wanted a real degree from a real university.

At long last, I stood up and prepared to walk across the stage. After twelve years of night school, I was going to receive my diploma. The master of ceremonies called my name -- ROBERT STAGMER. With steady, quick strides, accompanied by modest applause from my family, I approached the lectern. Grasping the parchment should have been exhilarating. Actually, I felt rather numb.

Graduation didn't mean the end of academic pursuit or the beginning of a new career. My career seemed already well defined and my further educational goals meant that this was only a stepping stone. My new priority was reaching for the top!

**My new priority was reaching for the top.**

I had already enrolled at the University to seek a Master's in Education on the way to a PhD. I coveted an advanced degree from a top university and now I was going for it.

Halfway into the Master's program, however, my perspective began to change. It was at this point that I became a Christian. The intellectual exercises that had once seemed so worthwhile now seemed more like so much busy work. I had expected a Master's program to be precise and crammed with excellent information. To my dismay, at least half of the courses contained 'Jargonized Junk'. I grew very disillusioned.

On the other hand, my new love had become the study of the Bible. Truths that I had learned as a child were coming back to me, and new revelations came on a daily basis. I was able to apply the scholarship techniques I had learned to my Bible study and many wonderful discoveries followed. It was a new kind of fun for me. I completed the Master's program only because it made professional sense to do so, but so much of the program had lost its appeal.

## WORSHIPPING GOD – MY PURSUIT TO THE TOP

The expression of my new found love came in a free exercise of the relationship that I now experienced with God. I simply could not get enough of spontaneous worship, seeking God's presence in song and shouting to him in exuberant fulfillment.

> **Spontaneous worship-seeking God's presence in song and shouting to him in exuberant fulfillment.**

## FOUNDATIONS

**Romans 12:1** 'I beseech you, therefore, brethren, by the mercies of God, that ye present your bodies, a living sacrifice, holy, acceptable unto God, which is your reasonable service.'

## WORSHIP IS LOGIAL SACRIFICE

The logikos, logic or reason, was elevated in Greek philosophy. It was thought that all things were done as a matter of reason. Man was a creature who committed his actions as an act of the will and the intellect. Life was a series of choices and the better, the more reasonable the choice, the better the man. In the Symposium, Plato quotes Diotima, the oracle, responding to Socrates, "I believe that all men do all things for the glorious fame of immortal virtue. The better they are the more they desire it, for they are consumed with the desire of the immortal." The ancient Greek felt that nothing should be left to ritual or compulsion. Ritual, blindly conformed to, robbed a man of his choice. Compulsion, on the other hand, brought out the banal instincts of lesser beings.

Latreia is the Greek word translated service. It could be a military term that describes obeying orders without question or a statement of the obligation of servitude. These two words seem to contradict each other when used together. "Reasonable service."

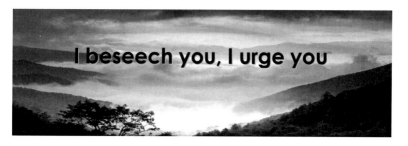

I beseech you, I urge you

## GOD'S LIFE

The Apostle Paul pleads, even implores us. He seems to be telling us for our own good, to 'listen up', to consider the great salvation that God, through his grace, has provided for us. We are compelled to respond with the only act that is appropriate. The only sacrifice we have to lay before His throne ourselves. The Greek for 'reasonable service' might be more accurately translated as 'logical sacrifice.'

When one harkens to Paul's cry in this passage, the individual finds it is a life changing and life ordering experience. Please, please walk in this. If he could, Paul would come to us, grab us and shake us and command, "WAKE UP! This is important; it is God's direction; it is

God's very life coming into your life. I beseech you, I urge you, brethren!"

## ACROSS THE THEREFORE BRIDGE

'...Therefore...,' Bob Mumford, a well-known Bible teacher, says, "When you see 'therefore' in the Bible, find out what it's there for!" Therefore is a bridge word. You need to know what is on both sides of the bridge in order to understand the full meaning of the passage. Chapters one through eleven of Romans tell us what salvation is, why it's necessary, how to get it, and once you have it, what it means. The remainder of Romans speaks of the results of salvation. Which side of the bridge are you on?

**Which side of the bridge are you on?**

'I beseech you, therefore, brethren...' When Paul speaks to 'brethren' specifically, to whom is he talking? Who are the brethren? He is talking to born-again believers; he is not talking to the world. It's one thing to talk to an unbeliever and say, 'You need to have your mind straightened out.' It is a far different thing to say to a believer, 'You have to get your mind transformed.' He is talking to us; he is talking to the Church. He is saying, 'Church, it is not enough just to make an emotional commitment; there is something further that must happen in you, Brethren...'

'I beseech you, therefore, brethren by the mercies of God....' What are the "mercies of God'? How does God demonstrate His mercies to you? By His great salvation. God makes an offer to each of us and says, 'here it is,' and He does it because of His mercy. It is a mercy that He bestows upon us by Jesus' payment of the debt that we owed on account of our sin, His punishment rather than our own deserved punishment.

You and I are the ones who should have suffered and hung on that cross. But Jesus did it for you and me. Jesus paid the price. "There is therefore now no condemnation for them which are in Christ Jesus.... For the law of the Spirit of life in Christ Jesus hath made me free from the law, of sin and death." (Rom.8:1-2). That is what Paul means by the 'mercies of God.'

## PRESENTING THE SACRIFICE

'...that ye present your bodies....' In the Old Testament, before a priest could worship, before he could lead the congregation in prayers and psalms and singing, before he could do any thing in the Temple, he had to present himself. He had to present 'the priest.' Before he could present himself he had to get clean, ritually clean. He had to get it right lawfully. The Priest had to enter the cleansing bath, known as the mikvah. The mikvah consisted of dual chambers where he would first scrub himself clean. When he was completely clean he would enter the second chamber which was the purification bath. The bather must fully immerse himself so that he was completely covered from head to toe. The mikvahs that I have seen were constructed so that the bather could stand upright and be totally immersed. Then the priest would put on' the 'inner garment' which was covered with the outer garment. This all had to be done before he put on his priestly apparel. At this point he finally was 'fit' to present himself to God.

The priest would go in to do the service before the Lord in the Holy place where he changed the bread and lit the candles and burnt the incense. Only he could be in there behind the veil. He wore bells on the hem of his garment which would enable the people to know he was alright as long as they heard the bells tinkling. The cessation of the bell's tinkling could possibly mean that something went wrong.

Zacharias, the father of John the Baptist, was in the Temple, ministering in the Holy of Holies (LUKE1:5, ff) when the angel came to announce that his wife, Elizabeth, would bear a son. Because Zacharias would not accept what the angel said, the Angel "struck him dumb". The people began to worry because he had been in the Holy of Holies so long. When Zacharias came out unable to speak they knew that he had had a spiritual experience.

We should be just as awe-inspired as those Old Testament priests were at the thought of coming before God. We must present ourselves to God. Worship is your first responsibility. No matter what else you do, worship must be number one. I do not mean public worship here. Church body and other corporate worship is good, and important, but your private worship, your worship when you are alone, your time between God and yourself is your first responsibility. Present yourself. This act is not an intellectual experience. It's not a spiritual experience in the sense that you can do it in the spirit and not in the body. The Word says '...present your bodies....'. This refers to your entire physical self. It's not talking about the flesh of your body. It's referring to the whole you. You must come into the service of God presenting your total self before His altar of worship. You cannot separate the intellect from the spirit or the spiritual from the physical. You talk about them separately but they are intertwined. Whatever the physical you does, the intellectual and spiritual you does also. If the physical you sins, the intellectual and spiritual you sins also. Present your whole self unto God. The wholeness of who you are must be presented unto God.

**Present yourself. This act is not an intellectual experience.**

## A LIVING SACRIFICE

Sacrifices were a part of the Temple worship. They would bring a lamb and use an extremely sharp knife. Theoretically, the sharp knife was supposed to cut without pain. They would bind the legs of a lamb, ram or bullock and slit its throat. The animal being sacrificed had no control over what was happening to it. By the time it was sacrificed, it was dead. Paul says to present your bodies a living sacrifice.

You are not dead; you are not out of control. There is no puppeteering going on. No one is yanking your strings. You perform this act of sacrifice with full knowledge. You present your life, with all its capacities, spiritual, intellectual, and physical, unto God. You do it consciously, and intentionally.

## HOLINESS OF GOD

"...Holy..." holy, holy, holy, holy, holy! What an important word! I think sometimes that if we would spend an hour and say nothing but the word "holy" we might get a little bit of an idea of what it truly means. Isaiah caught a glimpse of what it was all about (See Isaiah 6). It was on the Lord's Day, when he was in the Temple. He saw the Lord, high, lifted up, and His train filled the Temple. The seraphim flew around and there was smoke and fire.

John the Evangelist saw it also, didn't he? (See Rev. 1:10, ff) He saw the Lord and he was radiant. He knew it was Jesus; but it wasn't the Jesus he had known on this earth. It wasn't even the Jesus he had known in the resurrected body. This was a new Jesus, a powerful, mighty Jesus. He saw things around the throne he couldn't comprehend or describe. All this caused him to fall on his face as if he were dead.

Daniel saw it as well (See Dan. 8). He called the Lord the Ancient of Days, the glory and might of God.

Moses, of course, saw it too. (See Exod. 33:10-23) He was so overwhelmed by the glory of God that he couldn't even stand to look upon it. He could only look upon the hinder parts of God's presence as He passed by.

Adam saw it too. (See Gen.3:9-10) For Adam the experience was fearful because the state of his life was wrong. Up until that time Adam had walked hand-in-hand with God in the cool of the evening. When sin entered in, however, Adam could no longer stand the sight of God because God is so holy.

I'm sure that we don't have any comprehension of what the holiness of God really is. We need to gain a richer, fuller understanding. If we did so, we would be a transformed people. "Holy" means "separated unto God" it means "sanctified by Him," set aside for service, washed, cleansed from the contamination of the world.

## BAPTISM

Baptism is an important act. It has great spiritual significance in your life. If you have not been baptized as a believer you need to be. Jesus himself set the example for us. There is more to baptism than just getting wet. You are not just baptized into the water; you are baptized into Jesus, into His name. In baptism you are placed into (submerged, immersed into) all that his name is and represents. You are baptized in the name of the Father also, all that the name of the Father is and represents. Finally, you are baptized in the name of the Holy Ghost, all that the Holy Ghost is and represents.

We move into a new realm through baptism. It is the seal of the believer. Your Christian walk and life are not complete without baptism. In this act of obedience, you really do get cleansed. I have known Christians who were saved a long time but just couldn't get victory in their lives until they were baptized. Baptism is an aspect of God's transformation to take an unholy individual and clean him up. It helps make him a little more holy. The word *holy* also means a growing toward perfection in God. If your body is a holy sacrifice, then it's a sacrifice that is growing towards perfection.

## LOGICAL WORSHIP

Do you know what a home going word is? A home going word is one that tells you you're going to make it. As you get to those 'pearly gates' they will open up and let you come in.. *Acceptable* is such a word. You and I are acceptable to God, because we have accepted our Lord and Savior. Now He is calling us to do a little bit more. To be conformed to His purity, His majesty, His justice, His holiness, and to His love and mercy. That's what it means to be acceptable.

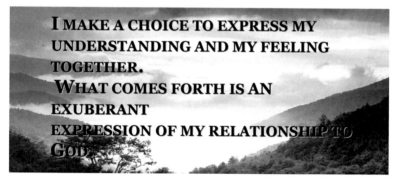

If we did so, we would be a transformed people.

The Apostle Paul explains that this '...is your reasonable service.' We need to learn to reason, to examine the pros and cons of an important issue. We have to be weighed in the balance. That becomes our reasonable service. The Greek word logikos is the root of our word logic. The Greek word for service is latreia, a hired servant who serves a master without question. This literally means 'worship.' When we combine logikos and latreia, we have logical worship.

**I MAKE A CHOICE TO EXPRESS MY UNDERSTANDING AND MY FEELING TOGETHER. WHAT COMES FORTH IS AN EXUBERANT EXPRESSION OF MY RELATIONSHIP TO GOD.**

My worship is done as a matter of my reason, an act of my will and my intellect; it is a choice, a decision. 'Which is your reasonable service'; You can choose to serve. As a hired servant you have already received your wages because, 'the wages of sin are death, but the gift of God is eternal life, through Jesus Christ our Lord' (Rom.6:23). The wages you now receive are no longer the wages of sin, but now you receive eternal life. Therefore, you have been 'purchased' and 'hired.' *You are now hired into service and your service is worship.*

My worship then is a combination of **obedient service** and **logical reasoning**. I make a choice to express my understanding and my feeling together. What comes forth is my exuberant expression of my relationship to God.

## SPIRITUAL INTELLIGENCE

1. What is the state of your spiritual intelligence?
2. Are you a creator?
3. Is worship your first priority?
4. Are activities of your life a sweet smelling sacrifice unto God?

It is now time for you to get in touch with the only source of real and lasting change.

Let's worship Him, our Lord Jesus Christ!

*Robert in Berlin, Germany at the Garden of
Charlottenburg Place*

*Robert & Annette at Home church in BERLIN*

# CHAPTER TWO

# Real Truth Brings Transformation

## THE IVORY TOWER

For several months I hid it pretty well. It wasn't that I was ashamed. I just knew that in the environment where I worked it wouldn't be popular. God knew I was hiding. Then it came. I was confronted with the choice that would cause me to unmask. I knew this moment was inevitable, but I was not prepared for the manner in which it came.

Several months earlier I had met Jesus Christ in a most dramatic way. My life had changed considerably. Yet I was carefully guarding my conversion where my professional life was concerned. You see I worked in a place where logic, knowledge, and reason were worshiped. God and Christianity were thought to be reserved for foolish women or so it seemed.

My field was educational administration. I had worked for over six years in the state education agency. The first five years had been as a data processing analyst in the Research division. As part of my master's work I had written an extensive analysis and futuristic recommendation for altering the distribution of state aid to education monies for the local subdivisions. When I shared the paper with my superiors they expressed sincere interest. Primarily because of my background in accounting and school finance (I had passed the C. P. A. exam some years earlier.). I was promoted into the Administration and Finance division where I was responsible for the multi-million dollar state and federal aid to education budget.

After five years of night school, I had finally received my bachelor's degree and now I was working on my

Masters. For the first time I felt like I was accepted as a professional in a place where the source and origin of your doctor's degree dictated the pecking order. However, I was not even on the entry level. I was mystified by the way the PhDs from the Ivy League colleges looked down their professorial noses at the DEds from State Universities. So I was not about to do anything to jeopardize my newly found staff acceptance by telling my colleagues about Jesus.

One Sunday night the pastor of the church I attended called me aside. It seemed that a Christian movie was coming to a local theater. The crusade organization that was hosting the showing of the film was looking for believers who could act as church captains to coordinate involvement. When the pastor asked me if I would serve in this capacity, I said, "Yes." When I got in contact with the organizing body, however, I discovered that what they really needed was a captain for the whole western quadrant of the city, extending out into the county. My job would involve publicizing and coordinating the involvement of two hundred churches. Personal visits in which I would show movie clips and distribute publicity posters had to be scheduled. Volunteers had to be organized and trained. Evangelism teams had to be recruited and trained for the nights of the movie showing. I loved it. Without hesitation, I dug in with my wife at my side. Eventually it dawned on me that my place of employment was in my territory. It occurred to me that my work place was the logical place to present the publicity for that geographic area.

I went through proper channels and reserved a room. That part was easy. No-one even tried to stop me. I put up approved posters announcing the day and time of the film-clip showing. People responded. Over forty people attended. Most were politely interested. By the end of the day I had even met several real Christians. So far, so good, I reasoned.

It took me several days to realize what was actually going on. The casual conversation that I was used to having with fellow employees vanished. The lunch table was filled by the time I got there. People stopped coming by my desk to talk. I was forced to eat my lunch alone or skip it altogether. When I entered a room where co-workers gathered, conversations hushed. The old topics of conversation didn't suit any more. My desk, which had often been a gathering place, was now a lonesome spot. Committee work that was once animated by joyful anecdotes became strictly business sessions. I sought out one of the Christians I had found working there. "Shirley," I said, "it looks like being a Christian in this place is a pretty lonely deal." "You're telling me?" She shook with a cynical laugh. "Not even the Christians stick together", I complained. "What we need around here is a lunch time Bible study," was her quick reply.

I considered her idea, fought it a little while, then I decided to give it a try. When I made the request for a conference room to use for Bible studies, every Tuesday from 11:45 am to 12:20 pm, it was granted without any problem so long as a work schedule or program did not preclude its use.

We began with five people in attendance. God gradually added people until at one point more than twenty people attended regularly! Several people accepted Jesus and lives were changed as faith came from hearing God's Word. As far as I know that group still meets in that workplace even though at this writing, seventeen years have passed. For a while it bothered me that our group was made up primarily of clerical staff, but occasionally one of the *professionals* would drop by.

My superiors changed my office situation giving me, a totally private area. I was the only person on that staff level who had a private office. I was allowed to furnish my office very privately and comfortably. I hung Phil Saint's painting The Way of the Cross Leads Home directly over my desk. In the lower right-hand corner there is a modern city in flames and destruction. Centered above it is the artist's conception of the New Jerusalem with a golden glow.

Separating the two cities there is a deep chasm filled with flame and smoke. The only way across the chasm is a huge white cross that forms a bridge for pedestrians to walk over the fiery holocaust. There are white-robed figures calmly strolling across the cross to safety.

People who would come into my office for business purposes would stop and stare at Phil's painting straight over my head. Nobody missed it. When their stupified silence became awkward for them, I would say, "Fascinating, isn't it?" Invariably, this would lead in to an opportunity for me to witness. Some even forgot why they came into my office in the first place. Others would almost run out as if to hide from the picture's message. A most memorable day came when one of the Ph.D.s came in, stared, listened, sat down and poured out his personal grief to me. His marriage and family were disintegrating. I shared God's word with him. This gave him encouragement. We prayed together. A few days later he returned, a far different person than the one who came into my office in the first place. He had obeyed God's Word; things in his life were on the mend. That was the beginning of my *personal counseling corner*. New friends, and some old ones, came by. They sought my opinion and my stand for Christ was respected. The professional status I had so enviously sought didn't matter any more. I was given a high-level assignment for developing certain top management strategies. I soon discovered that the two other staff involved in the assignment with me, were praying about the project. We prayed together. That assignment became one of my fondest memories.

## FOUNDATIONS

> Romans 12:2. "...and be not conformed to this world but be transformed by the renewing of your mind that you might prove what is that good, acceptable, and perfect will of God."

### Author's Paraphrase:

You are presenting yourself to God in worship as your first priority for the following purpose: *To not allow the conditions of this age to form you*. This present world is under Satan's rule. Remember that this world is only our temporary residence.

Do not allow external influences to shape you. Be recreated from within. Take on a change of appearance in the same way that God created life. Man was created perfect (before his fall in sin). Be restored to the state of Adam in the Garden. Your intellect, your powers of reasoning, even the knowledge that you have, will come as you are in unity with the Father and with the brethren. It is only unity of your mind (nous), with the minds and hearts of the brethren that will bring unity in the Body of Christ. Demonstrate by your actions and thought life what is morally honorable and well pleasing to God. Show forth the gracious designs of the Father. Be a delight and sweetness unto Him.

> Do not allow external influences to shape you.

### WHAT IS TRUTH?

We are given a command to 'be not....' Being is the state of life. Your state of life cannot be *conformed* by outward show to this world. This world is an illusion. I don't mean that the chair I'm sitting on is not real but rather that the principles of this world are an illusion. We all fall to their illusion. This world is under Satan's rule. It is dominated by Satan's perversion of God's principles. We need to remember that even our existence in this world is temporary.

Reality is revealed in God's Word. Jesus said, "I am the way, the truth, and the life. No man may come to the Father but by me" (John 14:6). Reality exists only in Jesus. Remember Pilate looking Jesus in the face and saying, 'What is truth?' He was looking at the only truth that would ever cross his path and he couldn't see it. He was conformed by this world.

**He was looking at the only truth that would ever cross his path and he couldn't see it.**

Paul talks about the rudiments of this world. (Col. 2.8) In the first century there was a Jewish heresy called Merkabah Mysticism. This teaching established a series of disciplines and religious rites which, when precisely followed, would bring the devotee to the point of having visions of God in His chariot. Today people still want to see visions and they do all kinds of things to get visions. Sorcerers (Rev.22:15) in Scripture is often taken from the Greek word "pharmacopeia" (or pharmakeus) from which we get the word pharmacy. It refers to drugs, most specifically hallucinogens. Such drugs are resorted to frequently by some wishing to have some kind of spiritual experience. Such people are not sure of what they are really seeking. No such activity will lead you to the Kingdom of God.

# CHANGED

'...but be ye transformed....' The Greek word used here is 'metamoropho'. It is the word from which we get metamorphosis. We use this word to describe the change of the butterfly from the worm—like caterpillar into a beautiful creature. The butterfly is also a beautiful symbol of the resurrection. We are to be transformed like the resurrection. One day I'll be physically transformed by Jesus. Until that time, I'll be happy to be spiritually and mentally transformed.

By what means are we transformed? '...by the renewing....' When we use the word *renew* we recognize that there must have been something there in the first place. It doesn't say get a mind or a new mind. It says get a renewed mind. In other words, there was something there to start with. There was judgment, perception, memory. We need to get it all renewed under the power and direction of the Holy Ghost, '...by the renewing of your mind...' Our brains have reasoning power, intellect, (sometimes called soul), and a will. We need to get our minds changed until they are under the influence of the Holy Ghost. We need to submit ourselves to the Holy Ghost, trusting that He will renew us until all we think and do, pleases the Father.

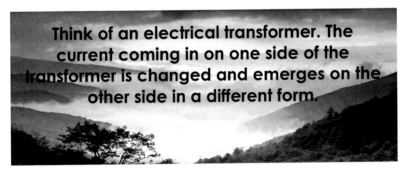

Think of an electrical transformer. The current coming in on one side of the transformer is changed and emerges on the other side in a different form. *It's still electricity, but altered to suit a different purpose.* The high voltage on the outside electrical wire would fry your household appliances. So, you use a **transformer** to change it into a useful voltage. You are not consciously aware of the change but you use it every day. The same electricity on that pole would have to be much more powerful for industrial applications. It can be altered to suit the intended purpose by voltage, watts, and phase. That is how God's word works in our lives. The power of the Word goes from the mind of the transformer - Christ- into our Holy Spirit sealed/indwelt mind and fits (renews) it for the purpose in God's plan.

## GOD'S WILL

Paul says that when our minds are renewed, renovated by the Holy Spirit, we will '...prove...'— we will demonstrate the will of God. We will show by demonstration who we are, what we are, what we do, by the way we live, by how we behave, by the company we keep, by the directions we take, by the service we give, what is good, what is morally honorable, what is pleasing to God, what is beneficial to ourselves and to our fellow man.

Perfect gives the true sense of being complete. Perfection is completion, being perfect is complete transformation, renovation. So many times we get involved with something and we can't finish it. We can't follow it through to completion. In Christ our being receives its end. We are concluded in perfection. This happens because the will of God is perfect.

How are such imperfect beings as us able to know the perfect 'will of God'? We know it through His Word. It is God's gracious design for all of us to be saved. The *thelo*, the delight and sweetness of God's perfect will, is revealed in creation and salvation.

Christians are creators. We are responsible in God to initiate a course of action rather than passively sit by and let circumstances do as they will to us. Are you being passive and allowing the world to shape you, or are you being active by the power of the Holy Spirit and the truth of the Word of God. You are responsible for the shaping of your character which is to be conformed to the image of God. You are responsible for submitting to God your character, which is to be conformed to the image of God, to Him alone who can conform it, who can renew it. **Our first priority is to worship**. It is God's good, and acceptable, and perfect will that we worship Him. Our second priority is to receive God's character from Him. In worship we draw close to God's very character. Knowledge of God's character requires intimacy. Intimacy requires that we worship Him.

Christians are creators. We are responsible in God to initiate a course of action rather than passively sit by and let circumstances do as they will to us.

No more guilt and no more shame,
No more tears and no more pain,
The world around me will not last.
All things are made new and the old all past)

I sing because I'm happy,
I sing because I'm free,
His Eye is on the sparrow,
And I know He watches (guards over) me.

*Robert prophesying from the Altar of Zeus in the Pergamum Museum in Berlin, Germany.*

"The German people will come to know that Jesus wept and that He weeps for them."

# CHAPTER THREE

# Giving God Joy

## MEETING GOD

I read a tract about meeting with God in the early morning hours. I had been a Christian for about a year when I read it. The tract convicted me of my need for a quiet time each day, so I began getting up early. I like to sleep, so it was really hard for me to exercise the required discipline. Years later, I must admit, it's still hard.

At the outset, I forced myself out of bed and dressed in my sweats to stay warm. Going into the family room, I turned on every light to help me stay awake. With my Bible on my lap and my glasses on my face I fought the good fight to stay awake and read the Word. I have to confess that many times I lost the battle and fell asleep in spite of my good intentions.

It didn't seem very spiritual, dozing off and waking with a start. I usually felt a little guilty about it. Slowly, however, I began to be able to stay awake a little longer. I was able to remember the word during the day. I decided to increase a half-hour to a whole hour. More fighting was required. I would read for about a half-hour and then pray. I began asking God to order my day. I took my Day Timer calendar book and made lists of the order of the day and assigned priorities in the day as I felt the Lord impressed me to do. As a result my days became less hectic. Things got accomplished. That year was the period of greatest growth for me.

## JEOPARDY

In the popular T.V. game, Jeopardy, one puts what he has at stake to gain winnings based on his knowledge and his ability to recall the correct information.

I love to watch Jeopardy and pit myself against the contestants. I do pretty well on most categories. I like the challenge of immediate recall.

How does that correlate to my relationship with God? The Apostle Peter says, '...be ready always to give an answer to every man that asketh you a reason of the hope that is in you...' (I Peter 3115.) If we don't have the right answer we may place ourselves in jeopardy of losing what we have. I have seen Christians who are at such a loss to explain themselves and their relationship to Jesus Christ that they begin to doubt. Paul says, '... I'd not have you to be ignorant, brethren....' I'd like to re-punctuate that phrase as follows: 'I'd not have you to be **ignorant brethren!**' As a teacher it is my job to see that we don't have any ignorant brethren. I want you to know what our faith is all about and who you are in Him.

How are you involved in giving God joy today? In what ways are you failing to give Him joy, thereby even placing yourself in jeopardy? I'd like to center in on the thought that abiding in an attitude of transformation produces a completion of joy. (See John 15:4-11.) Jesus says, 'If ye abide in me and my words abide in you...is my Father glorified.... ...that your joy might be full.' Abiding in Jesus is to get to know him personally. To know him you must know His word. As you do that your joy gets filled up.

# FOUNDATIONS

**Romans 12:3** "For I say through the grace given unto me, to every man - that is among you, not to think of himself more highly than he ought to think; but to think soberly, according as God has dealt to every man the measure - of faith."

## GRACE GIVES JOY

Everybody has their capsule definition of 'grace.' One of the most popular of these defines **grace** as unmerited favor. We didn't merit it, but we receive it anyhow. There's nothing wrong with that definition, except for it seeming to be less than full. I feel this way because the basis of the word that is translated as grace can also be translated as joy. This Joy relates to the giver as well as to the receiver.

In another of my own paraphrases, it could be stated, "By that which God has given me, which produces joy in Him, I might speak...." In other words, when I am moving in the **grace** that God has extended to me, in His giftedness towards me, it gives Him joy to give it to me, and in my exercise of what He gives, I produce joy in Him. I give joy unto the Father when I walk in His **grace**. When I walk in my natural character there is no Joy in the LORD, but when I walk in His **grace** and His giftedness, I also produce joy in Him. I give Him joy for I am reflecting His glorious **grace**! This is what the Psalmist means when he tells us to bless the Lord.

We see this same concept reflected in the following verses:

**Proverbs 29:3** 'Whoso loveth wisdom rejoiceth his father.'
**Psalms 149:4**, 'For the Lord taketh pleasure in his people.'
**Psalms 147:11** 'The Lord taketh pleasure in them that fear Him.'

We can produce joy in heavenly places, when we walk in His **grace** and His giftedness. How are you giving God joy today? Are you walking in God's **grace**, in the full knowledge that He has given unto you that which gives Him joy and calls you to walk in it?

**Heb. 11:6** says: "...without faith it is impossible to please God..." Therefore, I have to walk in '**grace**... through faith.' That's how we received salvation, in the first place; 'For by **grace** are we saved through faith. It is the gift of God, not of works, lest any man should boast.' (**Eph. 2:8-9**) God cares so much and wishes so much to produce joy in me that He joyfully gives forth to me and to every man 'the measure of faith'! God says that everybody gets it. Whether you exercise it or not is your choice. Everybody, who exercises faith in God's unique and only Son, gets the grace of salvation. God loves me so much that He provides, through His totally unmerited favor, a joy-producing quality, both in me and to me. It doesn't make any difference whether you are saved or unsaved. God's gift is still there for all to appropriate by faith. The problem is that as an unsaved person you cannot exercise it. Unsaved people cannot appropriate the gift.

We are under God's covenant whether we like it or not. He didn't ask us to be His people, He told us we are. He made a covenant with us and didn't ask or need our permission to do so. Now we can walk in agreement with the covenant and thereby receive the blessings which are the benefits of the covenant or we can turn our backs on the covenant and receive the absence of His benefits which is the curse.

## GRACE vs. PRIDE

Paul tells us, '...not to think of himself more highly than he ought to think.' If we begin to think of ourselves more highly than we ought to think, we commit the same error that Satan committed. He attempted to place his throne above God's throne (Isa. 14:13). I think Satan saw the empty throne at the right hand of God and thought it was for him and when he found out it wasn't, he rebelled. He wanted to exalt himself above Jesus and, therefore, above the Father. When we begin to exalt ourselves, to think more highly than we ought to think, we become like Satan who exalts himself.

We don't need to think we are equal to God or above Him, for that matter. Neither should we think ourselves above anyone else. I was not created to be your equal, nor am I called to be your equal. I am called to be a unique creation, a unique character in the Father. I don't need to be your equal. Neither do I have to be above you. When I am able to be me in God, what He wants me to be, I fulfill the maximum of my potential in Him by the exercise of grace through the gift package He has given to me. My gift package is unique. My temptations are the same as yours, but my gift package is unique.

I only begin to realize who I am when I stop looking at people around me and stop trying to copy their style. I realize that God has gifted me with a style of my own. I am my own person in the Messiah. When I actually understood these concepts, I began to actually like myself for the first time in my life. This did not happen to me until I was over thirty. It was then that I realized that I was somebody special. I could do unique things. My opinions, though they may have differed from others, were very worthwhile.

I always had a real problem in my life, especially in my professional life, because I always analyzed things differently from the way everyone else did. I was not wrong just different. Nonetheless, it always bothered me. I thought, "Why can't I think like they do? Why can't I come to the same conclusions that my boss does? Why am I always at odds with him?" It greatly bothered me because, essentially, I wanted to be an organization man. Yet I began to see that not only were my opinions worthwhile, but they were enlightening and fulfilling as well. God had gifted me in a unique way, even prior to my salvation experience, with insights other people don't have. 'PRAISE GOD!' and thank

God. I began to see that I could provide my part of the fullness of a group that could not exist without me. When I was not present people missed my insight.

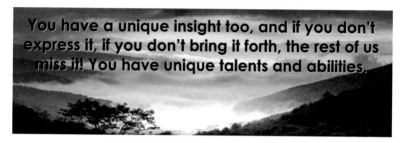

You have a unique insight too, and if you don't express it, if you don't bring it forth, the rest of us miss it! You have unique talents and abilities.

You have a unique insight too, and if you don't express it, if you don't bring it forth, the rest of us miss it! You have unique talents and abilities. You have unique giftedness from God. When you don't use them in the body, you leave a hole that needs to be filled and that only you can fill. There is a big gap of understanding, action, ministry, and ability when you're not there doing your thing, the thing you were created to do. No one wants to rob you of your individuality. You are unique in God. Be unique! You can be a unique individual and still be in perfect harmony with His Word.

If you want to be a maverick, if you want to be a character that stands out all on your own because you have exalted yourself too highly, that is opposing the Word of God. That's **PRIDE**. Don't think more highly than you ought to think. Watch it! **There is a need for you to think well of yourself.** If you don't think well of yourself you are not going to be worth anything to yourself or anybody else, least of all to God. , He loved me so much that He sent His Son to die for me, not us collectively, but for me, individually. God cares about this human being and His love is such that it is sacrificial towards me, individually. If no one else existed on the face of the earth, Jesus Christ would still have suffered and died for me. Appropriate that same truth for yourself. If nobody else existed on the face of the earth, Jesus would still have died for you! God could not stand to see you die in your sins with no possibility of redemption, without the possibility of a return to the Father.

## THE MEAT BETWEEN THE EARS

'Think.' Somewhere along the line, church people seem to have decided that they don't have to think any more. Just hold your hand up and close your eyes and you'll get a message. It's great when that happens! It does happen. I'm not putting down divine inspiration but God-gave you a *noodle* (a mind) up there to use and He didn't mean for it to be a 'wet noodle.' God gave us a usable, workable intellect. It's not just 'meat between your ears.' It is the residence of who you are. God gives you knowledge, understanding, and wisdom when you ask for it. The problem is, we don't ask for it enough! God expects us to use our nous (Greek for mind) and the major use we must make of it is to direct our will. I am responsible for directing my own will. My will does not control me. I control it. Say the following out loud: "WILL, I CONTROL YOU!" I am the author. I am the director. I have dominion over MY WILL. I make the choices. "So what about it? I will pray with my spirit, but I will also pray with my mind; I will sing with my spirit, but I will also sing with my mind." (1Co 14:15)

**When our minds are renewed we become the will of God in action.**

I must have a redeemed thought pattern also. My mind needs to be transformed by the renewing of the Word. My mind has to come into accord with God's Word directing my will and my knowledge, and my wisdom to do His will. Then I "Prove what is that good, and acceptable, and perfect, will of God." We demonstrate His will by what we are and do. We don't have to search around for God's will; it is us. His will is incarnate in us. God's will is revealed in His Word and when we are transformed according to His Word, we act according to His will. It is then that we show the will of God to the world. "For the earnest expectation of the creation waits for the manifestation of the sons of God" (Rom 8:19).

## BEING SOBER

Not collectively, but privately with God, each of us must examine ourselves so that we don't "think of ourselves more highly than we ought to think." We need to think soberly of ourselves. In this context, sober means more than the lack of an intoxicating beverage. Paul uses sober to point out that there is a revelation of knowledge that enables me to discharge the ministry God has placed within me. Being sober means I am able to see clearly that which God has given me and called me to accomplish. That calling demands a clear and steady perception from me of my calling and my circumstances, and also from you in your calling. We need to get the fuzziness out, to clean out the cobwebs. We need to get our vision clear. I also need to have sober judgment about myself. "To thine own self be true, and it shall follow, as night follows day, thou cannot then be false to any man." Shakespeare wrote that; it's not in the Bible. If you are true to yourself, you cannot be false to God.

## MEASURING FAITH

**Rom 12:3** ends with this: "According as God has dealt to every man the measure of faith." We all have a measure of faith. The word according means following through to. We must follow through to the fact that God has dealt to every man the measure of faith. How do you measure faith? James says, "Show me your faith and I'll show you my works." If I have faith I must be doing something with it. Faith can be measured by the fruit it produces. In order to be a fruit producer or a faith-works producer, we have to grasp the gift that God has placed within us. That measure of faith is the measure of how much I trust God.

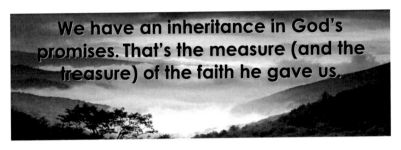

We have an inheritance in God's promises. That's the measure (and the treasure) of the faith he gave us.

One thing about the Jews of Jesus' time, and even the Orthodox Jews of our time, is that they have trusted God and God's faithfulness. The nature of my spiritual gift is such that nothing in this word eludes me. It has been said that there are over six thousand promises that God has made to His people, and every one is available to me. Every single promise is mine. The fulfillment of those promises is God's problem.

He made the promises to me and to you, and we must learn what they are. We have an inheritance in God's promises. That's the measure (and the treasure) of the faith he gave us.

The measure is not a thimble-full, or a cupful. I can't quantify it with a ruler or a scale. The only way you can personally measure it is by the promises and how they come about in your life. What is your life producing? Show me your faith and I will show you my works. You say you have faith; you confess God's Word; you see the Word active in your life. How well does Cadillac faith (that's the kind of faith that can believe for a great financial blessing) work in a foxhole? There's nothing wrong with Cadillac faith. I'd like to drive a Cadillac. I believe that Christians should be prosperous. We should confess every prosperity promise every day. Prosperity is an important aspect of faith and we cannot overlook prosperity. However, the important thing is knowing the promises of God and acting expectantly in accord with them.

There's another side of faith that's necessary as well. When you are down in a foxhole experience and people are shooting at you, you're being talked about, lied to and cheated on, and it is then that you had better know how to rest in God's promises. It is then that you'd better have the kind of foundation in faith that saved David and countless others in their lowest hours, in their times of great troubles.

Annette and I were very excited about the vision God had given us to start a Christian school. We were excited and scared. Though we knew it was in conflict with the direction of the church we were attending, the first person we told was our pastor. We believed that God works through His delegated authority. So, we told the pastor, half expecting a rebuke. Instead He told us that he could not confirm or deny the vision. He suggested that we should go to the Christian persons in the body that we knew would tell us "no" if God was not in it. We were to explain our vision, pray and see what they said.

We knew exactly who to see. Although we respected this brother and his wife, and the depth of their walk with the Lord was well known to us, we always seemed to be on the opposite side of every issue. We called to ask for an appointment and one was cheerfully granted. The meeting began with prayer. Then I explained that God wanted us to establish a new Christian school founded on the principals of individualized education. When I finished the brother took off on a tirade about the evils and ills of the local Christian schools. I glanced at Annette and could tell that she had the same sinking feeling that I felt. Yet, as quickly as he had begun the brother stopped and turned to me saying, "But what you are talking about is right." Another Christian brother who was present began to speak words of prophecy about how God was going to establish this new ministry. The meeting ended with us all joining hands and the former adversaries praying prayers of confirmation over us. Through the many troubled years of founding and developing the Christian school we could always look back and know that the vision had been confirmed according to God's authority and the direction given to us through our pastor.

Faith through grace brings joy to God.

## **PRAY WITH ME.**

Father, I know that as I walk in the grace you have already given me I bring you joy. Help me, Father, to increase my little faith that I may be a person of your promises. Lord, transform me according to your Word and let it be a permanent work in me. Help me abide in your loving work and grace that I may demonstrate your purposes. Cause my life to inspire others to desire and come to know you and to value your worth. Cause them to see that they can, may, and ought to please you; to give you joy by being acceptable, holy, living sacrifices to you. Help me to put my Christian thought and action to use that your Kingdom may come on earth as it is in heaven. Amen.

*Robert in Berlin blowing shofar in front of the Reichstag.*

# CHAPTER FOUR

# Rejection

## SEPARATED? ALONE?

Have you ever felt the pain of separation and being alone? Has it been difficult for you to seek out and share your problems with a brother or sister in Christ? Has a sense of rejection been plaguing you? Often our own aloofness is the very cause of our being alone. God does not intend for it to be that way. God says that we are members one of another. He means for us to be linked together in life and service. As we contribute one to another we become joined in a relationship of mutual benefit in the Lord. He doesn't mean for us to lose our individuality, but rather to find fulfillment in submerging our independent status into a unity with others which knows no separation. We are to be in unity. The Hebrew word for one is 'yachad'; to be one as God is one. There is no disagreement between the Father, Son, and the Holy Spirit. In the same way, "How good and pleasant it is when brothers dwell together in unity" (Ps. 133:1). The corollary is how ugly and awful it is when brothers disagree. Unity, then, is the next phase of bringing joy to the Father we will consider, that we may participate in the unification of His body on earth.

## FOUNDATIONS

**Romans 12:4-5** "For as we have many members in one body and all members have not the same office; So we, being many, are one body in Christ, and every one members one of another."

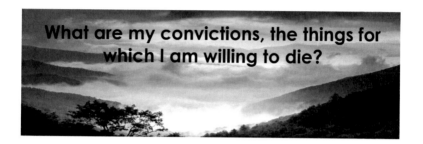

**What are my convictions, the things for which I am willing to die?**

## THE BODY

All of believing Christianity is one body. Regardless of the label we may wear, we are one body. We don't need to get caught up in nuances of doctrine where we disagree. There are a lot of things that can rub you the wrong way about some segments of Christianity. Nobody in 2,000 years has come up with the whole truth. The only ones who have had the whole truth are cults. One major mark of a cult is that they claim to have an exclusive on the whole truth. Although I study, check out doctrines, and believe that my principles are well-founded, I must keep on asking, "What are the essentials? What are my convictions, the things for which I am willing to die? Which principles are such that I can stand back and willingly allow others to believe their own way?"

We need to keep a proper perspective on essentials. One of these is relational maturity. I don't have to be a perfect mirror image of you, a perfect jigsaw puzzle fit to you, to know, work, and associate with you. I cover your faults, you cover mine. I cover your weaknesses; you cover mine. I can share your strengths and you benefit from mine. When we are concerned with relational maturity, we can avoid arguments over tangential doctrines that are not essential to salvation and Christian Life. I can relate to someone who may hold elements of doctrine with which I do not agree, for the purposes of the Kingdom of God. We need to covenant together for the mutual purpose of the spreading of the Gospel. Pastor Fred Lessans quotes Saint Augustine, "In essentials unity; in non-essentials diversity; in all things charity."

We are one body in Christ yet '...we have many members...' You are a unique person. No one wants to rob you of your individuality. My little finger, for example is what it is, and there is no other finger like it. It has a unique purpose and a unique function. Without my little finger I am missing something. Similarly, my thumb is a thumb that is unique to me as a human being. Did you know that monkeys don't have thumbs? We are the only animals with a thumb. Monkeys have five fingers and must curl their hands in order to grasp an object. One physical feature that makes man unique from all other animals is the thumb. Without our thumbs we loose a major capability of our body.

One time I broke my little toe. Usually, I never think about my little toe. I don't give it any consideration at all. Most of the time, it is the last part of my body that gets any conscious consideration whatever. When I broke that little toe, my whole body felt it. The pain of the break was bad enough, but afterwards, I had to shift my balance in order to walk without pain. This affected my right hip and my left shoulder and I got a 'crick' in my neck and my head started to hurt. I couldn't think and I didn't want to read. Nothing worked right when that little toe wasn't working the way it was supposed to work. Now, who would have thought that such an insignificant part of the body could debilitate the whole person?

It is the same in the Body of Christ. When a brother or sister (even one who sits in the corner and prays and never says anything or never seems to do anything and is ignored most of the time) is missing, the body hurts. Most of the time we may not even realize what the source of the hurt is.

## IDENTITY IN THE BODY

Everybody is unique, but we are of the same body. Presently, there is an identity crisis in Christianity. Some may say, "Don't call me a Pentecostal because they do funny things in their services." Another person might demand, "Don't call me a Charismatic because they have had bad publicity lately." Then someone else puts in, "Don't call me a Fundamentalist because that doesn't sound intellectual enough." It is not hard to imagine someone saying, 'I don't want to be called an Evangelical because they don't have enough freedom." Then there are those who declare, "I don't want to be from a mainstream church because they are bound up in tradition."

**Brothers and sisters, we are having an identity crisis.**

Brothers and sisters, we are having an identity crisis. But we are all Christians if we are saved by the blood of the Lord Jesus Christ. Wherever God has placed you, as long as you know He has placed you there, be content. There may be a time when God calls you to separate. Make sure it is God calling and not some aspect of your flesh. When you do separate do it decently and in order. Even if you are uncomfortable for the moment, that discomfort may develop qualities in you that God couldn't get to otherwise. "Iron sharpeneth iron" (Pr.27:17). Nobody likes to hear that verse. It is true none-the-less. We need to know who we are. We need to say, with a certain sense of inner satisfaction, that this is where God has placed me and this is the body of which I am part.

## OFFICES

In the Body of Christ there are different "offices." The New King James and The New American Standard use the word **function** instead of office. I think it should say opportunities to serve. That's more in line with Jesus' words – "If you want to be great in the Kingdom, first be a servant." God has established certain very specific duties, and responsibilities among the people whom He has called to represent the Body of Christ on earth. There are differing offices in God's Government. I believe that God has a ministry for every person who is willing to fill it. If you are willing to walk in the grace, that which gives Him joy, God has a ministry (maybe a better word would be mission) for you to fill. Everyone is a minister and has a mission. However, God gives certain persons as gifts to the church to walk in His Governmental calling.

There can only be one head. Anything that has two heads is double-minded and is tossed to and fro. There are many positions to be filled. Responsibility and authority come with an appointment to an office. We have to be very careful that we do not think of ourselves "more highly than we ought to think." This is especially true when we begin walking in the responsibility and authority of an office. When a person starts to elevate his individual area of service, he or she runs the risk of offering "strange fire" unto God rather than an acceptable sacrifice.

Don't confuse appointment to a specific service area with a gift. God may give you the gift of prophecy but that does not make you a prophet. A prophet walks in the calling and anointing of an office. Just because you happen to prophesy in a meeting, don't start wearing a hair coat or eating locusts and wild honey. I do know prophets who are called to that office and become ministers to the Body of Christ. Such individuals are called and gifted, not with an occasional 'anointing' but, with a permanency. It is important to realize that when a person is gifted, a calling may be on the way also. We have to look for that. We must also know the difference between the anointing and the appointing. My friend, George often said, "Man appoints and God anoints." Too often we appoint a person to fulfill an office who is not anointed to that office. The result is, at best, difficult. We should recognize the anointing and let the appointing follow. We walk together as a body with our various anointing, calling, and giftedness. Paul admonishes us to walk in grace, considering what God has done. We need to accept our anointing as being a work of the Lord in us and through us <u>for others</u>. In so doing, we produce not only joy in our walk but also joy in the Father, because the gifting emanated from His joy in the first place.

How are we falling short, failing to give Him joy, even placing ourselves in jeopardy?

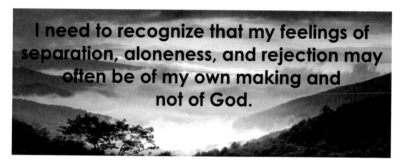

I need to recognize that my feelings of separation, aloneness, and rejection may often be of my own making and not of God.

## STEPS TO UNITY

First of all, we are not going to be integrated with the body in the way He has called unless we are part of it. The Word is clear on this. **There needs to be a conscious joining, not just a failure to join or separate.** I need to invest myself in the ministries of the Lord Jesus Christ. If I wish to produce joy in the Father I will join together with my brothers and sisters. By His grace this will cause my direction and their direction to be joined together in a way that fulfills the ministry God has called into existence.

Secondly, I must never elevate myself to any position or status. I produce humility and humbleness by allowing myself to be who I am, never getting an exalted opinion, of what I have thought or done. If I get a vested interest in my ministry I may get very protective about it. What I produce as a result is not freedom but restriction. .

Third, I need to see that whatever I contribute is not of me, but is through me by the grace of God. A failure to do this negates faith. The minute I put "**I**" in the center, I become a victim of "I worship." That Is **I**-dolatry.

Fourth, I must invest myself in the development of the unity of the Body of Christ. I need to recognize that my feelings of separation, aloneness, and rejection may often be of my own making and not of God. My own failure to integrate myself into the whole of believing Christianity produces separation. By investing myself, I move in fulfilling His vision and calling. The Body of Christ is all-inclusive, made up of contributing units, each unique, distinctive, and important, linked together for life and service. Each belongs to the other, not working independently, but profiting from each other's contribution to the whole. Each member belongs to the other. Together all will profit in many ways through our contributions to the whole. By remaining separate, by working independently, we will not profit as we certainly will when united in the Lord. The "glue" that joins this laminating of gifts and calling is the desire to bring joy to the Father.

## PRAYER FOR THE GIFTS AND CALLING

Father, help us to submit ourselves to your calling and gifts so that in an integrated exercise of worship and service, we exhibit your body to a dying world.

*Robert in Sherwood Gardens, Baltimore, Maryland*

# CHAPTER FIVE

# Gifts for the Body

## LORD, LORD

Jesus asked the question, "Why do call you me, LORD, LORD, and do not the things which I say?" (Luke 6:46)

As I read \ Romans chapter twelve, verse five and six, it is my conclusion that in order to contribute to the Body of Christ, each member is gifted. These gifts operate according to the personalities of the ones who are gifted. The degree of giftedness each individual possesses is according to the Father's grace which produces joy in the giver. We are gifted with special abilities beyond the natural talent we possess individually and uniquely for the benefit of the whole body. Our use of these gifts is for the purpose of edifying (to strengthen and encourage).

## FOUNDATIONS

**Romans 12:6-8** "Having then gifts differing according to the grace that is given to us, whether prophecy, let us prophesy according to the proportion of faith; or ministry let us wait on our ministering, or he that teaches, on teaching; or he that exhorted, on exhortation; he that gives, let him do it with simplicity; he that rules, with diligence; he that showed mercy, with cheerfulness."

The gifts listed in Romans 12 are given to individuals <u>at birth by the Father</u> and determine the nature of the individual. These are innate (in born) in every person regardless of belief. They are your personality DNA. These are the "Charismata"; they enable a person to walk into his destiny in God. A failure to identify and walk in these gifts will produce failure in life and a missed destiny. When I say destiny in God I would explain it this way. God has a plan. (See: I Cor.2:9, Eph. 2:10) He knows you. There is a place and calling for your life that is predestined. However, you have to find that place. You have to discover who you are and your calling. Then walk towards it. This is how I define my free will. When you get there will depend on the nature of your walk. Many people never get there or get there late in life. Others arrive early in life and achieve a form of greatness in that position. We need to recognize our gifts and direct our life towards their fulfillment.

The seven **Gifts of the Father** are listed in these passages. In my opinion this is not a closed list but rather a representation.

1. prophecy
2. ministry
3. teaching
4. exhortation
5. giving
6. ruling
7. mercy

If you observe closely you will see that in the broadest sense these gifts are exhibited in all walks of life.

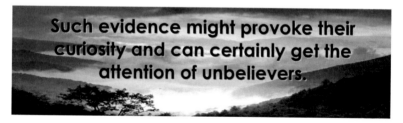
Such evidence might provoke their curiosity and can certainly get the attention of unbelievers.

## NO IGNORANT BRETHREN

In First Corinthians chapters 12 and 14 the **Gifts of the Spirit** are thoroughly discussed. Paul tells us that he would not have us "ignorant, brethren, (Remember about ignorant brethren.) concerning spiritual gifts". These gifts listed in this scripture are the **manifestation gifts** and are given to show <u>the presence of God in our midst</u>. The controversy in the Body of Christ should not be over whether gifts operate and if so which ones. But, rather the question should be, why do we so seldom see the scriptural gifts in the fullness of operation that the body so sorely needs? Jesus asked the question, "Why call ye me, LORD, LORD, and do not the things which I say?" The gifts are for the body and they operate in and under the authority of the body (I COR 14:26-33, 40). Signs and wonders operate outside the body primarily as signs for those who would come and believe. A demonstration of gifts does not bring people to salvation. Such evidence might provoke their curiosity and can certainly get the attention of unbelievers.

## **PROPHECY**

In the scriptures, prophecy is given to unbelievers and the disobedient to warn them of coming destruction. Unbelievers don't usually like to hear about their destruction. With the notable exception of Nineveh, unbelievers don't usually pay attention to prophesies of destruction. Jonah didn't want to tell the inhabitants of Nineveh about their destruction. He was afraid that they would listen to him. One theory says that they were the enemy and he wanted to see them destroyed. He knew that if those people did listen and did turn and repent that God would not destroy them. Did you notice in the story that Jonah never told those people to repent? I think he didn't want them to repent.

Now try that. Go down to the local disco and tell the people in there that their destruction is coming. You will be thrown out on your ear. They are certainly not going to fall down and repent. They might give you a bumper sticker; they will try to convert you. The party mentality wants joiners. It is a warning to be heeded, but unbelievers usually ignore or reject it.

Prophecy to the body is for edification. We define prophecy as the gift which allows one to clarify what is happening now and what is about to happen through the Lord's grace. It builds up the body; it strengthens the body; it is confirming; it's nothing new; we already knew it or suspected it. Prophesy can be segmented in two parts:

1. To forth tell – That is to expound on the gospel
2. To foretell – What the Holy Spirit says is going to happen

## TONGUES

To the unbeliever the gift of tongues is usually confusion, baby talk, babble, drunkenness. Unbelievers don't understand tongues; a message in tongues is no sign to them at all. Actually, it tends to increase unbelief. However, in some situations, the tongue is actually a language that the unbeliever knows, such as in the book of Acts when the Holy Spirit fell on the upper room. In that case the scripture says that the multitude heard their languages being spoken. Please note, it does not say that the languages were actually spoken but what was heard. What would it sound like if one hundred and twenty people spoke at the same time in ten or twelve different languages-BEDLAM. So how could they have heard their own language and understood it? It had to be supernatural hearing,

Tongues to the believer are a sign of the power of God moving in that individual. When the interpretation comes through the body, the body is lifted up. On one occasion we were praying at a church with a pastor and her intercessors. During the evening at one juncture we divided up into twos. I was paired with the Pastor. As we prayed I began speaking in tongues. As I finished a sequence I looked up and saw the astonished face of the pastor. "Have you ever been to the pueblos in the Southwest?" She asked. "No." was my answer. "Well you were speaking in a perfect native American dialect from that area. I know I spent several years

46

there as a missionary." "What did I say", I asked. "You were speaking the praises of God. You even had the right intonations and tones."

## HEALING

Healing is usually seen by unbelievers as mind over matter. Jesus performed only a few healings, and no miracles, where there was no faith. Where there is no faith in operation, few miraculous things will be seen. The exception is when a witness is accompanied by the authentic operation of a gift. We have seen street ministry be extremely effective when accompanied by healing. That can really get the attention of an unbeliever and cause them to question.

## AUTHORITY

When you are operating in the gifts in a body, you need to be under the spiritual authority of that body. Paul tells us that the gifts are to operate decently and in order. God is not the author of confusion, but He is the author of peace. Authority and order within a body should allow for the operation of gifts. When gifts are operated in a body but not under the authority of that body they may lead to confusion and disruption. If you cannot operate your gifts within the authority of the body either you are operating incorrectly or you don't belong in that body. Lets say that you have a prophetic word that you think is for the body but it is critical of some aspect of the operation of that body. It is wise to submit that word to leadership before any public utterance. They may suggest that you wait and make a private appointment to discuss this word with the pastor. If the leadership does not allow that word to be given at all, the responsibility is on them.

## ORDER & RESTORATION

The body of which you are a part must be in order and have discipline. This means that when someone is in error the guidelines of Matthew Chapter 18 must be followed.

Step 1 is to go to the party in error, one-on-one, in humility.
If they accept you, you have won a brother.

Step 2 is to go again with someone the individual will respect.
If he now hears you, he is restored.

Step 3 is to take the offense before body authority.
If the party in error hears, he is restored. If he will not hear, then he is to be excluded.

We must keep in mind that the end product of discipline is always restoration. It is also a tireless process that must be followed through to perfection. Peter asked, "How many times must I forgive my brother?" Jesus answered, "Seventy times seven." He didn't mean four hundred and ninety. He meant forgiveness is unto perfection or limitless. In other words, forgiveness is the kind that leads to restoration. Jesus told us to do it by the spirit of the law not the letter of the law. Don't appropriate some narrow verse to the exclusion of the whole of the Scriptures. When we go to a brother or sister in love to give attention to some kind of problem situation, we must never go in condemnation but rather in a spirit of restoration. If the attempt is rejected, we owe it to that person to take the next steps, even to the point of bringing it before the body so that real restoration can occur. (See also Gal.6:1-2). B


## ASCENSION GIFTS

### Ephesians 4:7-16

"⁷ But to each one of us grace was given according to the measure of Christ's gift. ⁸ Therefore He says:

*"When He ascended on high,*
*He led captivity captive,*
*And gave gifts to men."*

[9] (Now this, *"He ascended"*—what does it mean but that He also first[c] descended into the lower parts of the earth? [10] He who descended is also the One who ascended far above all the heavens, that He might fill all things.) [11] And He Himself gave some *to be* apostles, some prophets, some evangelists, and some pastors and teachers, [12] for the equipping of the saints for the work of ministry, for the edifying of the body of Christ, [13] till we all come to the unity of the faith and of the knowledge of the Son of God, to a perfect man, to the measure of the stature of the fullness of Christ; [14] that we should no longer be children, tossed to and fro and carried about with every wind of doctrine, by the trickery of men, in the cunning craftiness of deceitful plotting, [15] but, speaking the truth in love, may grow up in all things into Him who is the head—Christ— [16] from whom the whole body, joined and knit together by what every joint supplies, according to the effective working by which every part does its share, causes growth of the body for the edifying of itself in love."

These <u>Gifts of the SON</u> are given to the body for the body. Their purpose is **to train up the saints for the work of ministry;** not to be the only ones doing the ministering but to train up others. <u>They are not positions or descriptions of a hierarchy</u> but they are servant gifts to the body for **government and training.** They are to guide the body into unity of the faith and protect it from unsound doctrine. Those gifted in these manners will guide and direct the body into its destiny.

Jesus demonstrated this principal by first training the twelve, empowering, and releasing them to minister. He did the same with the seventy. On the job training while doing the ministry should be our pattern.

## MULTIPLICITY OF GIFTS

What we find here is three different categories of giftedness - one from **the Father**, one from **the Son**, and one from **the Spirit**. I used to think, based on incomplete teaching, that these were simply redundant lists of the same nature. However, they are three different lists given three different ways for three different purposes. They are not exclusive in that they work together. Think of a cube. On the front face of the cube write the Romans gifts. On the side write the Corinthians gifts and on the top face write the Ephesians gifts. See how these intersect? There are 7 in Romans, Nine in Corinthians and four (or five) in Ephesians. Do the math.

That is 7 X 9 X 4= 252 possible combinations. However, taken one at a time or two at a time or three at a time... we get permutations of over 4,000 different **gift sets** or what we call **gift packages**. Thus you can see that gifts will manifest very differently depending on how they interact with each other. For example, a pastor/teacher who is gifted prophetically and with administration will act very different from a pastor/teacher with a gift of mercy and healing. The same applies to a prophet, an apostle, or evangelist.

## BODY COMMITMENT

There must be commitment to the body so that we can endure a time of discipline and grow. To be a disciple you must bring yourself under Godly discipline. We all need to be accountable to someone whether it is an individual or a collective.. If there is no commitment, the first time discipline is in order the subject will just cut and run. Then the person will go and talk about "how awful those people in that church are." Watch it when someone comes to you and starts talking about how bad those people are on the other side of town. If they are talking about them now, six months from now they will be talking about you. Don't get caught in their trap. If you have ought against a brother or sister you must go to them. <u>Remember restoration is the goal</u>. It's all built upon body ministry and supernatural understanding. If we operate in the flesh we will mess it up. There has to be a commitment that says, "I belong to this body of people. I love this body of people. I will stay with this body of people and I will restore myself to this body."

If the body is in error, it is my job to try and restore it. If and only if the local body strays into the path of sin, and will not hear, must I separate myself from it. Even then I must make an attempt to tell them (at least twice according to Titus). I am affected by what they do. Even when I cut myself off from that body I am affected by what they do. I carry a spiritual stigma until that body is restored. I've lost something of the Body of Christ if that body or that individual or that group gets lost. I've lost something. I've lost a piece of me that could have otherwise been functioning. I've lost talents; I've lost resources. I've lost the potential of that group to move with the fullness of the Body of Christ. It's like having a cancer. We need to restore our fallen members, and stop talking about them. If we don't heal our fissures they get infected. We must suffer the discipline of the Lord in order to grow.

Sometimes I have known discipline in my life that has come from the Body of Christ. My first reaction was to get up and run, shake the dust off my feet, and say, "They're unfair. I'm getting out of here!" God would not let me do that. I've had to grow, deal with my own feelings, go back and apologize even when I didn't think I had a whole lot for which to apologize. In that, God has made me to grow. It's a commitment to the body that's necessary.

## BODY STRENGTH

If we look closely at **Matthew 18:15-20**, we will notice that several times there is a call for unity. Verse eighteen tells us that we shall bind and loose on earth and correspondingly it shall be done in heaven. In verse nineteen we are told to agree and in verse twenty we are told to gather together in His name. It is stated in the Scriptures that the unity of a husband and wife is necessary so that their prayers not be hindered (I Peter 3:7). So it is that the unity of the body is necessary, that our prayers be not hindered. When we are unified we have strength that multiplies.

Leviticus 26:8 tells us that:
1)Five can put 100 to flight.
2)One hundred can put 10,000 to flight.
Following that progression:
3.) Two thousand can put one million to flight.
(5X20=100, 100x100=10,000,
100x20=2000, 10,000x100=1,000,000)
In number one above we see that each member is handling twenty.
In number two each member is handling 100
In number three each member can therefore handle 50,000 -
God blessed them and told them to be fruitful and multiply.

If we are not in agreement, gathered together, joined fitly one to another, braided together in an unbroken cord, then we can't pray in faith, believing. We lose the power that Jesus promised us as a body. Why aren't our prayers being answered? Maybe we had better look at the body and see how together we are, see how much agreement we have. I certainly don't mean agreement over genealogies, contentions, and points of law, that's vain according to the Letter of Titus. I'm talking about being together in the Spirit of the Law, the Law of the Spirit of Love in Christ Jesus that frees us from the Law of Sin and Death (Rome 8:1). We do not have to think alike in the fine points of doctrine. We are free to disagree, but we are not free to sever our unity. You do not have to think just like I do to be in unity with men. You do not have to share my strain of theology, but you should be moving in love with me. Christians are initiators not reactors.

## THE THINGS I SAY

Now let's look at Matthew 25:31-46. Why does He call those people and separate them this way and that? Look at the things He says about them:

> When I was hungry, you fed me;
> When I was thirsty, you gave me drink.
> When I was a stranger, you took me in.
> When I was naked, you clothed me.
> When I was sick, you visited me.
> When I was in prison, you came to see me.

**We are free to disagree but we are not free to sever our unity.**

Jesus said the same kinds of things in the Sermon on the Mount (See Matthew 7:21-23). Jesus said that He needs us to do these things. He cannot do them while He is seated at the right hand of The Father; He needs us. Jesus is making intercession for us. He is not up there begging The Father to do something. He is actively intervening – taking an active role – in the situation on our behalf, so that we can be directed by Him in our actions. We are His body here that must do these works of ministry. Our ministry is to reach out, to touch lives, and to be salt in the earth. In the illustration of the sheep and the goats, the goats were living by the letter of the Law. They didn't see Jesus, so they didn't do the things He said. The sheep on the other hand, didn't see Jesus either but they did follow His teachings anyway because they weren't trying to be legalistic. They were just doing what He said.

## TRUE RELIGION

What is true religion? "Pure religion and undefiled before God and the Father is this, to visit the fatherless and widows in their affliction, and to keep himself unspotted from the world" (James 1:27). To visit the widows, the orphans, the infirmed, the imprisoned, that is true religion. **Are you tired of practicing a phony religion?** I've visited the prison a few times. I've seen that a few needy people got clothing. We took some food bags to hungry people. It has been a long time since I had a stranger in my house. I pray for the sick and I have seen some dramatic healings.

**The question I need to ask myself is**, "What do I do with my spiritual gifts?" **Jesus said, Matthew 10:7-8 (New King James Version) "And as you go, preach, saying, 'The kingdom of heaven is at hand.'** Heal the sick, cleanse the lepers, raise the dead, cast out demons. Freely you have received, freely give."

What is He going to say? They said, "When did I see you, LORD?" He makes it pretty clear what is expected of us if we are going to call Him "LORD." "But I cast out a demon, Lord. There was a demon here last week, and I cast it out. Wasn't that good LORD? LORD, I anointed the sick with oil and prayed for them, some even got healed, LORD. I've been out witnessing, LORD." Will He answer, "Depart from me, I never knew you..."?

How much influence does the world have on me? (**Romans 12:2** "...be not conformed to this world...") He wants me to be unspotted from the world. Fortunately for us Jesus has some good spot remover. It's called confession and repentance. So when we do realize that we are going the world's way instead of His, REPENT. He is quick to forgive.

We need to realize that the one thing He wants the most from us is our personal relationship with Him. We need to walk and talk with the Father like Adam did in the garden. Our first priority must be worship. I must be converted unto Him. Then, and only then, do I begin to walk in the directions He has given me. We are going to be called to task for our obedience in this Christian life. We can't say LORD, LORD unless we will do what He says. And what does He say?

Feed the hungry.
Take in strangers.
Clothe the naked.
Heal the sick.
Restore the sight to the blind.
Visit those in prison.
Care for widows and orphans.
Cleanse the Lepers.
Raise the dead.

*Robert in Germany at the garden of the Kaiser's Palace in Charlottesburg, Berlin.*

*Robert with Intercessors, praying at the nation's capitol*

## AN ACTIVE BODY

This is the vision of what the Body of Christ must be about. We must be an active body ("each joint supplying"). If we are not an active body we are a dead body. A dead body decays and wastes away. An active body grows and strengthens. Pure religion and undefiled, that's what our body must be.

**Your citizenship is in heaven. You have a heavenly culture now and you are a new creation.**

Oh, yes, He says one more thing: "Keeping ourselves unspotted from the world." That means not letting ourselves get conformed by the external circumstances. That's what we mean when we talk about holiness. We must reevaluate our involvements in things that do not lead to holiness.

> If the only funny movies use bad language, don't watch them.
> If your crowd does drugs, get out of it.
> If the styles make you an exhibitionist, don't wear them.
> If the music is ungodly, don't listen to it.
> Do not be a support to one of these because the person or persons belong to your race or culture. Your citizenship is in heaven. You have a heavenly culture now and you are a new creation.

In the long run a compromise with the world is never worth it. If we become spotted by the world we are no longer a sacrifice that is acceptable to God. Remember, worship is our first priority.

## HAVE FUN

Please don't get the idea that the Christian life is full of negatives. Satan's realm is the realm of negatives. *Christ's*

***kingdom is the realm of positives.*** He told us what to do in a positive way. Don't get the idea that being a Christian isn't any fun. Somehow, when you are doing God's will and giving Him joy, He returns the joy. Christians who actually pursue the will of God have more fun. The great thing is that this kind of fun is never destructive. It builds up the individual and the body. Worldly 'fun' always has its destructive and dangerous side. It might be fun for a while but it ends in sadness. That is a result of satanic perversion. Christians may have to go through difficulties but God always turns their sadness into joy when they are in His will. Those who follow Satan go from joy to sadness while those who follow Christ go from sadness to joy. Again we are presented with a choice! We may either initiate joy by following Jesus or be satanically controlled and destined for sadness.

## PRAYER FOR UNITY AND POWER

Father, we thank you and bless you for your Word active in our lives. It challenges us to be an active moving people for you, for no other reason than the fact that you told us to do so. Lord, help us to be that ministering people, to come into that strength of unity and commitment, to be in order, to be moving in authority. Help us, LORD. Help us to be the representation of your body, with signs and wonders following. Empower us, O GOD. Thank you, LORD, that we are a people who are transformed for victory.

# CHAPTER SIX

## Believing is seeing.

### BELIEVE GOD

Have you ever heard the saying, "Seeing is believing?" I want you to know that the opposite is true, believing is seeing. No one really believes something because he sees it. Believing comes first. In Acts 19 Paul met some Ephesians who were believers but they had not yet seen the baptism in the Holy Spirit. They were baptized with John's baptism which was a baptism of repentance. They had not heard of spiritual gifts; they had not heard of the Holy Ghost. It is not even clear that they had heard of Jesus or the Gospel.

> These people did not believe because they saw it happen, they saw it happen because they believed. They simply believed God.

When these twelve men heard that they should believe on the Lord Jesus Christ, they were baptized in the name of the Lord Jesus, 'and when Paul had laid his hands upon them, the Holy Ghost came on them; and they spoke with tongues, and prophesied' (Acts 19:6). These people did not believe because they saw it happen, they saw it happen because they believed. They simply believed God.

There is no evidence that they received any teaching or information concerning the spiritual gifts before they received them. They believed God, and the gifts came by His grace. These gifts were evidence to the body of the infilling of the Spirit of God in these believers, and evidence to the believers themselves of the miraculous move of God they experienced.

My uncle, who passed on at the age of eighty, was a Methodist minister and evangelist. His wife, my aunt, was a deaconess who ministered at his side for nearly sixty years. They were special people. When you walked into a room in their presence, you just knew they were so special. A wonderful love and joyfulness exuded from their being. They didn't even have to say anything they just glowed. I knew that they were 'born again' because their testimony was ever on their lips.

When I met the Lord and received the Holy Spirit and the Gift of tongues, I wondered how they would take it. I had never heard them speak of anything besides salvation so I was pretty certain that they weren't going to accept my experience as valid. Annette and I took my mother to meet my aunt and uncle and leave her to spend a few weeks with them. I made up my mind that I was going to tell them about my experience at this encounter. I loved them very much and was fearful that this might be a very cool reception.

After we arrived I said to them, "Aunt Sarah and Uncle George, Annette and I have something to tell you." Without waiting I continued, "We have been born again, and received the Holy Spirit and we also have the gift of speaking in tongues." With the most pure honey smile and that lovely southern drawl Aunt Sarah spoke first, "Well now Honeys, we've been doin' that for years."' It seems that some years after they were saved God miraculously gifted these two lovely people. They hadn't sought the gift. It just came. They believed it was from God and accepted his sovereign work. They didn't preach it because that was not their calling.

Annette's mother and sister lived in Dallas. On one of our trips to visit the family, they introduced us to a little, old lady who had been born in Mexico. She had been a Roman Catholic all her life. I'm not sure I remember her name but let's call her Rosita. A few months prior to that meeting, Rosita had attended a meeting of the large Catholic charismatic community there in Dallas. In the course of time she had been baptized in the Holy Spirit and had received the gift of tongues. When she had told her parish priest about the experience, he, at first, treated her with disdain. He charged her, "Well, let me hear what you said." Rosita simply opened her mouth and, in faith, began speaking in other tongues. The priest's shocked look told her something was wrong. 'What's the matter, Father?' 'Where did you learn that?" was his reply. Rosita, responded with a question of her own "Learn what?" "What you just said." came the answer from the still shocked priest. "I don't know what I said, I was speaking in tongues. What did I say?" she said, and it was her turn to be mystified. Noticeably shaken the priest responded, "You said 'Praise the Lord' in my native tongue of Lebanese." This is why we can say tongues and all the gifts are operating today, and cannot be ignored. The evidence is too compelling.

From that initial experience the priest began a quest that led him to that same gathering of Charismatic Catholics where he too received God's gift of Holy Spirit. With a renewed commitment and power in his spiritual life that man is now ministering elsewhere and spreading the wonderful experience he has found for himself.

## FOUNDATIONS

**Romans 12:7-8** 'Or ministry let us wait on our ministering or he that teacheth, on teaching or he that exhorteth, on exhortation, he that giveth, let him do it with simplicity; he that ruleth, with diligence; he that sheweth mercy, with cheerfulness.'

## GIFTS

Ministry is the act of serving, meeting the needs of others without any thought of self benefit. As we wait on God we begin to understand our interdependence with others. For example, we see how our gift(s) that were given to us by God are used for the welfare of others so that the whole body benefits. We realize that such gifts are supernatural endowments rather than natural talents or abilities. We also use our natural talents for God's purposes. The combination is what makes us unique in our ministering. We willfully place our selves at God's disposal to do His will rather than our own.

The gift of teaching enables us to instruct in the nature and character of God and His Word. We begin with the basic foundational teaching of the Apostles, the Kerygma, the teaching and doctrine upon which all teaching hinges and against which all teaching must be judged. The Kerygma has five basic points:

1. The Messiah of Old Testament Prophesy has come.
2. Jesus Christ is that Messiah.
3. Jesus died on the cross. He died willingly. It was God's plan. He was a substitution for our sins.
4. Jesus was resurrected.
5. Jesus will return.

There are many other truths to be taught but they must always return to the foundation laid by the apostles. If you examine every sermon and epistle in the New Testament you will always see the the Kerygma is the essential framework.

We are told to exhort our brothers and sisters. The purpose of exhortation is to encourage and to provoke them to love and to good works. Our exhortations must follow the example of Jesus and the apostles

1. Witness
2. Baptize
3. Make disciples
4. Form churches
5. Teach
6. Exhort, rebuke, correct, encourage
7. Train them as ambassadors of Christ.

8. Send them out to witness, baptize, heal the sick, and make disciples.

## TITHING AND GIVING

One should give or contribute to the body of Christ and one should do so joyfully and liberally. This should include church expenses of the congregation you attend. Some people do this through tithing. Tithing is 10% because it means 10%. (See Malachi 3:10) If your taxes are figured on your gross income shouldn't a tithe be based on the gross income as well? The tithing or offering is to come from the first fruits of your labor or increase.

We have examples of tithes and offerings before the Law was given. Abraham's tithe to Melchizedek and Abel's offering are two such cases. Abraham's tithe of 10% was taken from **the spoils of war**. He did not keep the other 90% of the spoils but gave them to the King of Sodom. So it is difficult to compare current day's teachings on tithing to this scriptural reference.

**However,** it is noteworthy that in the New Testament starting with the Acts of the Apostles, there is no mention of the New Testament churches tithing. Tithing was held as a law and there were temple taxes in addition that were required. Jesus came to fulfill the law so that we were set free to express our love for Him and our brothers and sisters . If 10% was required before Jesus, wouldn't it stand to reason that with His very own Spirit in us **we would well exceed the giving required by the law**?

Jewish people were schooled in the tradition that if you had a rabbi who discipled you, then you gave to his support. What is emphasized throughout the New Testament is their generosity in liberally giving to the needs of the churches which were in need in other regions. Such is the case cited in *II Corinthians 8:3 & 4*. Paul states that the Macedonian Churches begged him to receive their offering while they, themselves were in need. **Giving** is referred to in this passage as <u>fellowship with a part of the body of Christ in another region.</u> In v. 8 Paul emphasizes that this is an **encouragement** to give generously and <u>not **a command**</u>.

## INTO THE STORE HOUSE

Where do I give it? I used to teach that the tithe (which was taught in every church) goes to your local church. If you want to give elsewhere then you would give beyond the tithe. I no longer fully ascribe to that as an absolute. The scripture says "…into the storehouse…" So what is a storehouse?

If the local church is where you receive your ministry and is providing your spiritual development, then, give it the whole tithe or **support offering**. Are the ministries of that organization proving to be a storehouse where believers are prepared for the work of ministry? Are new believers cleaned up, filled, taught, and given opportunity to serve? Then give the full support offering. If the answer is no, then you should seek the Lord if it is His will for you to stay there. If it is, ask Him for a strategy to see your storehouse set free into its New Testament assignment.

There are promises and blessings that go with giving but that is another subject. Give simply and cheerfully. Always give as secretly as possible (don't get hung up if your act becomes known, but don't do it to be known). Give liberally with NO STRINGS ATTACHED. BE SURE TO SEEK GOD AND HEED HIS VOICE. Not every 'CHRISTIAN CAUSE' is your responsibility. If you go to hear a speaker, be ready to give a special offering. Ask God how much, but don't skimp. When you support a prophet you reap a prophet's reward. In the Bible, we learn that people always took care of the prophets. Those who did were taken care of by God meeting their needs.

Jesus told His disciples that they were not to rule over each other as the heathens do but that they were to be servants. When a brother or sister is placed in a position of authority, the purpose is to bring God's order, discipline, maturity, and earthly perfections into the lives of the members of the body. As such we come to the aid of each other. Such tasks should be discharged with zeal and earnestness while at the same time being mindful of Christ's sacrificial love. I think that the most desirable gift is mercy. Through this gift we are able to comfort and encourage the human soul. Mercy may be the most misunderstood characteristic of God. Yet it is most essential.

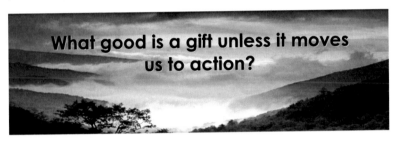

What good is a gift unless it moves us to action?

## MOVED TO ACTION

In **Romans 12:7-8**, we see that ministry is referred to as a gift while the action that follows is the action of ministering. If believing is seeing, as we have stated, then seeing means that we will be provoked, moved to action. Today, too many believers get talked out of their gifts. A new believer has all kinds of faith to believe. "Faith cometh by the hearing and hearing by the word of God' (**Rom.10:17**). Disbelief comes as a result of the traditions of men. Jesus rebuked the Pharisees by saying that they were 'making the word of God of none affect through your tradition,' (Matt. 15:6, Mark 7:13). In many instances believers, whose spiritual eyes are just beginning to open through the word of God, are talked out of spiritual gifts and powerful ministry by men who are tradition bound. These tradition bound men go outside the Word of God, failing to rightly divide the word of truth (II Timothy 2:15). The reason they are so bound is they fear that these empowered believers will up set their carefully constructed religious tenets. One of the arguments advanced against spiritual gifts is that they were only for the apostolic age to be used in the establishment of the Church. The Word of God, however, never says that. Another tradition uses this verse: 'But when that which is perfect is come, then that which is in part shall be done away' (I Corinthians 13:10) to discount spiritual power today. They insinuate that the gifts are imperfect and the Word of God is perfect so the gifts, therefore, have passed away. James tells us, 'Every good gift and every perfect gift is from above...' (James 11:7). Now I certainly agree with the perfection of the Word, but scripturally I cannot accept the argument that the gifts are imperfect and therefore have passed away.

**Today as in the days of the Apostles, perfect gifts are given to imperfect people.**

The gift that generates the most controversy, yet is referred to as the least of the gifts, is glossalalia or speaking in tongues. The Apostle Paul says, "I would that ye all spoke with tongues..." (1 Cor.14; 5), and "forbid not to speak with tongues..." (1 Cor. 14:39). In churches where speaking in tongues is an accepted spiritual gift, new believers often receive this gift at the same time they receive salvation. Other times, because our society is so spiritually inhibited (bound up), new believers require additional ministry to become open to the indwelling presence of the Holy Spirit and spiritual gifts. When I received the Lord Jesus, although I was in a church that accepted all the spiritual gifts, I did not immediately speak in other tongues. Several months later, as I was praying, I realized that I was speaking in other tongues. I don't even know how long I had been praying that way. It was just a very natural and expected empowerment. In the same way I have experienced other spiritual gifts in my life. No emphasis or striving need be placed on the gift. Just believe. Believing is seeing.

# BELIEVING

Believing is seeing GOD in personal awareness.
Believing is seeing GOD in the world and creation.
Believing is seeing GOD in people who are no longer strangers.
Believing is seeing GOD for ourselves.
Believing is seeing God.

When we first believe and our lives are changed, we have no doubt it was God. Every element of our being witnesses to the fact that a supernatural act has taken place. We simply would never have submitted our stubborn wills to the surrender that is required in salvation without it being supernatural.

As we begin to study the Word of God for ourselves our understanding is quickened and we see things that we could not grasp before. The Holy Spirit of God makes the Word alive, whereas before it may have seemed only to be confusing literature. As we receive the indwelling presence of Christ through the Holy Spirit and great changes begin to work in us and our everyday lives. We see the moving and empowering of God. We pray for the sick and injured and see them healed. We give someone words of personal prophesy. We lead someone to Jesus. We disciple, we teach a new believer. As we recognize the availability of spiritual gifts that enable us to work beyond our natural abilities, we see God with us. As we submit ourselves to the discipling process through other Christians and allow the Word to become part of our intellect, our minds are renewed, the old things pass away and all things become new. We add to our personal testimony. It is then that we see God. Believing is seeing God personally.

Believing is seeing God through the world and creation. **Romans 1:19-20** tells us that all creation speaks of God and that man has no excuse for not seeing it. I love the outdoors. I like to stand on a mountain and survey the panorama. The variety of terrain, flora and fauna that can be seen in the day and the expanse of the universe at night testify to my Creator. The order, despite the complexity and variety of creation, speaks of a super intelligent Creator. The theories of chance and happenstance just don't hold up. Yet unregenerate man continues to invent and substantiate so called scientific theories to explain creation.

Anyone who has studied the history of scientific paradigms, models, and theories realizes how easily they are destroyed. Only the creation story of Genesis has withstood the test of time. Yet the seeing does not produce acceptance of the Creator Being. On the other hand, when a person becomes a believer he sees and knows the truth of God's Word and the hand of the Creator. Believing is seeing God as creator in His universe.

Believing is seeing God through people. Somehow when you become a believer you no longer regard people as strangers to be ignored. You begin to see people as God sees them. People are in need of a Savior. This is the reason why God empowers us to be witnesses for Him (Acts 1:8). Where formerly we would have been embarrassed to introduce ourselves to strangers, much less talk about God, if we allow God to take over now we will care more about winning a soul for Jesus than any possible embarrassment. We will see that person as perishing in the fires of Hell unless we intervene with the gospel. If Jesus doesn't get him back, Satan will get to keep him. We are moved with compassion towards that unknown individual. This is the key to an on-fire Christian life. A witnessing Christian is a Christian growing in spirituality and in truth. **A non-witnessing Christian may become ingrown, develop all kinds of troubles, waver in belief, and perhaps even fall away.**

As we continue in our spiritual growth, we begin to see strangers as lonely and deceived people, in need of a real friend, and in need of the truth. The best thing we can do is to introduce them to Jesus and then be a real friend by leading and discipling them. Every one is in need of a family.

Many people today are estranged from their natural families. Bringing a person into the family of God fulfills a need in their lives. Ministering to a stranger through the power of God by signs and wonders and seeing that individual transformed before our eyes into a brother or sister in Christ is seeing God.

Believing is seeing God in our own person. Nobody knows me as intimately as I do, except God. Nobody knows the person I was before meeting Christ the way I do. Nobody knows the changes God has wrought in me like I do. It has been suggested that every Christian should write out his testimony as a legacy to his children. If you can't write, speak it into a tape. Our testimonies make good tracts that help us to lead others to Christ. But I think that even more important, we need to review our testimonies for ourselves. It helps us to keep from losing our first love. When we recall where we were and how far we have come, we know that God had to be involved.

God wants intimacy with us. When we meet Him personally and privately, He will speak with us and minister to us and we will know that we have met God. Failing to meet God in this way, we may grow cold. Remember that worship must be our first priority. We need to stir up the gift within us (2 Timothy 1:6). The empowerment of God from within is evidence that God is active in our lives. Believing is seeing God in ourselves.

## PRAYER FOR SEEING

Lord, open my eyes that I can see you in all my encounters. Help me to be personally aware and guide my thoughts. Let me see you in your creation, in people and in

> We need to review our testimonies for ourselves. It helps us to keep from losing our first love.

myself. And God, please stir up my heart with your passion for witnessing to strangers and others around me. AMEN

# CHAPTER SEVEN

# Loving God Is A Full-Time Job.

## EXCITEMENT

About one year after I accepted Christ, I went through a time of intense searching for the love of God. I knew from the Word that I loved God and that He loved me but I just was not experiencing it. It didn't seem real. I reviewed my salvation experience. I knew that was real. I just didn't seem to be able to enter into a real love experience with the Lord. My head told me every thing was okay, but my heart and my gut weren't satisfied.

Sometimes I'd just sit and tell God I had to know His love for me; I had to feel it; and to experience it. Seemingly to no avail I cried out in my spirit to touch what I knew was there but could not find. My wife, Annette, had met the Lord only a few months before I had and she seemed to walk in a protective surrounding of His love. I was jealous, envious, and frustrated. I'd only been married for about a year and six months and my love relationship with my wife was really growing. We had done a lot of changing since meeting Jesus and our relationship seemed like courtship all over and it was exciting. I knew that loving God was different but I also knew that it could be just as exciting. But it wasn't happening for me; I wasn't excited about loving God and I wanted to be.

## MESSIANIC JEWS

It was a cold, blistery evening with ice and snow on the ground, the winter of 1973. Annette and I had decided to attend a meeting of Messianic Jews in Silver Spring, Maryland. The speaker that night was a born-again Jew named Art Katz. We were totally unprepared for what happened during the meeting. A segment of the large, excited crowd booed, hooted and catcalled.

They applauded in all the wrong places. The crowd of largely Gentile Christians was stunned to silence and confusion by the brash rudeness of the hecklers. Art Katz seemed to take it all in stride as though it was to be expected. At one point he explained that the J.D.L. was present and that we should pray that the Word of God would penetrate their already solidified hearts. Until that time, I had never heard of the J.D.L. Later, I was to find out that these young, rather affluent—looking Jewish men were from the Jewish Defense League (J.D.L.). They were sincere, conservative, and orthodox defenders of Judaism. Threatened by Art Katz's testimony, they thought he was there to destroy them. Sid Roth led everyone in prayers for these misled defenders from the traditional Jewish community.

During the preliminaries of the evening, after a rousing and soaring time of opening worship, a young man came to the podium. He read from I Cor. 13. As he spoke, 'Though I speak with the tongues of men and of angels...,' his face seemed to radiate. I was drawn to this young, happy man with what seemed to be a golden aura around his beaming face. The words of love pierced down inside my spirit as never before. God was telling me that He loved me, and that He received my love for Him. The swelling inside my chest seemed to take over my whole person and I felt that special warmth and thrill inside. I looked at my wife, choking back the tears of joy, and said, 'I love God and He loves me, and I really know it.' I have never met him in person, but, someday I want to thank Larry Tomczak for his testimony in Scripture that dramatically met a need in my life that night.

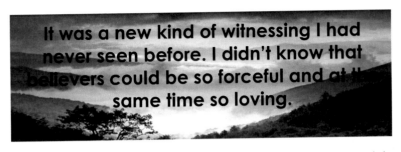

It was a new kind of witnessing I had never seen before. I didn't know that believers could be so forceful and at the same time so loving.

Later that evening we saw love at work as the Jewish believers confronted the J.D.L. The raging young traditionalists spat hot words in the faces of the peaceful even joyful believers. The believers listened patiently then countered with words of love, peace, and faith from the Jewish Scriptures, literally challenging their detractors to look at the printed words on the pages. At times it seemed almost as if violence would erupt, but thankfully it didn't. The large groups began to break down into one-on-one discussions; sometimes the interchanges were heated and at other times they were civil. We learned later that several of the former adversaries became believers that evening. It was a new kind of witnessing I had never seen before. I didn't know that believers could be so forceful and at the same time so loving. That night I entered into a new dimension of GOD'S LOVE. You see, loving God is a full—time job.

## FOUNDATIONS:

**Romans 12:9—10 'Let love be without dissimulation. Abhor that which is evil; cleave to that which is good. Be kindly affectioned one to another in brotherly love; in honor preferring one another'**

From Wikipedia, the free encyclopedia

**Dissimulation** is a form of deception in which one conceals the truth. It consists of concealing the truth, or in the case of half-truths, concealing parts of the truth, like inconvenient or secret information. Dissimulation techniques include: camouflage (blend into the background), disguise appearance (altering the model) and dazzle (obfuscate the model).

Dissimulation differs from simulation, in which one exhibits false information. Dissimulation commonly takes the form of concealing one's ability in order to gain the element of surprise over an opponent.

## THE GREAT COMMANDMENT:

Jesus said that the first and most important (greatest) commandment was to love God with your whole heart, soul, and mind (might), (Matt. 22:36-38). Did you realize that the love commandment is not in the list of the Ten Commandments? While we're on the subject, do you know what the Ten Commandments are? Do you know where they are found? Read them in Deuteronomy 5:7,8, 11,12, 16-21 or in Exodus 20:1—17. Most people can't name all ten and few people know where to find them in the scriptures. Jesus points out that the most important commandment was not even in the original ten. It comes from Deuteronomy 6:5. It is part of the SHEMA ISRAEL, the 'Hear, 0 Israel' passage in which God speaks declaring what will be right for the people to do in the Promised Land when they possess it. If you read carefully you will see that the following passages detail what it means to love God with everything you have.

1) Verse 6 - Keep His words in your heart.
2) Verse 7 - Teach His words to your children.
3) Verse 8 - Keep His word before you always.
4) Verse 9 - Write them on your door posts.
5) Verse 12 - Don't forget where you came from.
6) Verse 13 - Fear, serve Him, and swear by His name.
   (take your oaths-NIV)
7) Verse 14 - Don't worship any other Gods~
8) Verse 16 - Don't tempt God.
9) Verse 17 - Keep His commandments (all of them).
10) Verse 18 - Do that which is right and good in the sight of the lord.
11) Verse 20 - Tell your testimony to your sons and daughters.

Now remember that, today, we do these things not out of any sense of obligation or fear of reprisal, but out of LOVE for God. Don't get hung up in legalism. Salvation is free. Loving God, however, is a full—time job. Jesus said, 'If ye love me, keep my commandments.' He also said, 'If a man love me, he will keep my words' (John 14:23). He went on, 'This is my commandment, that ye love one another, as I have loved you' (John 15:12). In another verse He promised, 'If ye keep my commandments, ye shall abide in my love' (John 15:10). Abide means to live or live in. Later, he said to Peter, 'Lovest thou me?' He went on, 'Feed my lambs' and 'Feed my sheep' (John 21:15-17).

## THE SECOND COMMANDMENT

Jesus continued His declaration by saying that the second commandment was like the first, 'Thou shalt love thy neighbor as thyself.' That one is not in the Ten Commandments either. It comes from the order of conduct for the Levitical priesthood that is found in Leviticus 19:18. It is not unlike the Golden Rule that is found in Matthew 7:12. It's virtually the same as John 13:34-35, where Jesus said, 'A new commandment I give unto you, that ye love one another; as I have loved you, that ye also love one another. By this will all men know that ye are my disciples, if ye have love one to another.' He commands us to love as He loved. That is Agape love. It is love that is not interested in self, that has no thought of personal gain or return, but thinks only of the welfare of the other person. . .

When we commit ourselves to loving God, we commit ourselves to a life of study and prayer also.

The Golden Rule does not guarantee reciprocal behavior from those whom we are serving. Rather we are told to treat others the way we would like to be treated, not necessarily in the way we are treated. If followed unselfishly, this rule does often generate such reciprocal behaviors. That, however, is not the point to be considered. We love others because we love Jesus, not because we are coerced to do it and not for any thought of reward or avoidance of punishment, but we do it purely because we love Him. It is our love, expressed to the other for their benefit only, which distinguishes us from other people and labels us 'disciples,' and followers of the Lord Jesus Christ. In truth, I know many believers, born-again Christians, but I don't know very many disciples. Sad isn't it? Loving God is a full-time job.

**In order to really love God we have to invest ourselves with our whole heart, soul and mind.**

He said that if we loved Him we would keep His words and observe His commandments. That is quite a statement. It means that first we have to know His words and commandments. It means we have to read and 'study to show thyself approved unto God...'

(2 Tim. 2:15). We have to know the words and commandments in order to keep them. When we commit ourselves to loving God, we commit ourselves to a life of study and prayer also. Without prayer we cannot get the fullness of meaning that the Holy Spirit brings to the Word. Our prayerless reading becomes a lifeless intellectual exercise devoid of God's inspiration.

This knowledge of the Word is also necessary so that we can fulfill the commission to teach our children, feed the lambs, and feed the sheep. We must know the words of God in order to write them on our 'gates and door posts' and to keep them ever before us. For us to relate our testimony to our sons, and anyone else for that matter, and for it to have power, it must be reflected against and in agreement with God's Word. Only His Word is guaranteed not to return unto us void. Our words have no guarantee, but His Word is always fruitful (Isa. 55:11). The scripture says that we overcome by the words of our testimony (that is in alignment with His word) and the blood of the Lamb.

There is no substitute for a systematic study of the Scriptures. Most people don't have the discipline or academic background to do this on their own, so we see many ministries conducting a variety of courses and this is as it should be. Too few Christians avail themselves of these opportunities. In order to really love God we have to invest ourselves with our whole heart, soul and mind. That means there is going to be some real effort involved. Loving God is a full—time job.

## EVERYTHING HANGS ON LOVE

The third thing Jesus said was that on these two commandments hang all the Law and the prophets. ALL of the Law and the prophets hang on LOVING GOD with ALL our heart, soul and mind and UNSELFISHLY LOVING OUR BROTHERS. The combination of all the Law and the prophets is actually the whole of the scriptures. Therefore, He is saying that the whole Bible is about LOVE.

That shouldn't really be so revolutionary. The greatest verse of the Scripture, if one can really be called greater than another, is John 3:16 which simply tells us how great God's love toward us actually is. "For God so loved the world, that He sent His only begotten son ..." *(into mortal flesh to suffer and die and thereby thoroughly satisfy God's wrath for the sins of those who believe).*

The logical conclusion is that in order to really know about and experience all the love that we can have for God, and He for us, we must study all of the scriptures. Anyone who has attempted to undertake any biblical scholarship knows that it is virtually impossible to learn everything that is known about the Bible. You could never read all the books that have been written or listen to all the sermons that have been preached. Today    biblical research, archeology, and scholarship are more prolific than at any other time in history. You will soon realize that though you might spend a lifetime exclusively studying the Holy Scriptures you could never learn it all. You see, loving God is a lifetime job.

# CHAPTER EIGHT

## Staying Alive

### BUTTER COMES FROM CREAM

I loved listening to Dr. John Garlock. He was associated with the Christ for the  Nations Institute in Dallas. Dr. Garlock has been heard to quote this 'piece of doggerel', as he referred to it: ( according to one source it was originally written by by T.C. Hamlet.)

Two frogs fell in a pail of cream, or so it has been told.
The sides of the pail were shiny and steep.
The cream was deep and cold.
'Well, what's the use?' said number one.
'It's fate, no help around.'
'Good bye, my friend, Good bye, cruel world.'
And sighing still he drowned.
But number two, of sterner stuff,
Dog paddled in surprise,
While he licked his creamy lips and blinked his creamy eyes.
'I think I'll swim a while,' said he, or so it has been said.
'It really wouldn't help this world if one more frog were dead.'
So he paddled on for hours   and was never heard to mutter.
And then hopped out from the island he had made
Of fresh churned butter.

Sometimes the situation in which we find ourselves seems as hopeless as it did to frog number one. The sides are too steep; the pail is too deep; the cream is too cold. The only thing left to do, it seems, is to give up. The thick and soupy situation that seems like crud could turn out to be cream. Just the very act of staying afloat could create the path of escape, by refining the cream into an island of butter. That which may seem to be our demise could actually become our salvation. When we get in the tightest and most difficult of situations the temptations to revert to the former ways of life are often so great. Frog number one fell into the trap of thinking that inaction was a solution. Frog number two, on the other hand, simply looked at the situation and decided not to be controlled by it.

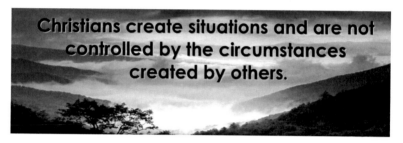

Christians create situations and are not controlled by the circumstances created by others.

The point has been made that Christians are to be initiators, not reactors. Christians create situations and are not controlled by the circumstances created by others. We are a people, transformed for victory. We have read the end of the book and we have discovered that WE WIN!!!

> We win; we win.
> Hallelujah, we win!
> I read the back of the book,
> and we win!

REPEAT THAT SEVERAL TIMES TO YOURSELF (OFTEN).

## FOUNDATIONS

**Romans 12:11—12** 'Not slothful in business; fervent in Spirit; serving the Lord; Rejoicing in hope; patient in tribulation; continuing instant in prayer;...'

## REKINDLE

When we are initially converted, at the time when we are born again, when we come to the altar and confess the

Lord Jesus Christ as our Savior and our Lord, when we determine that our life is now given over to the new pattern which is the Lord Jesus, an instant glow and ardor emanates from our being. Sometimes it gets us into trouble. Sometimes it's misunderstood. Persons come up to us and ask, 'Has something happened to you?' 'Have you just met Jesus?' 'Have you had a spiritual experience?' We wonder, 'How did they know? Have they seen something in my face or did they just sense it?' God seems to do such miraculous and amazing things for us. He opens the Bible to just the right Scripture when we need it. He gives us the right word to say at the right moment, beyond our own knowledge and ability. He sets up situations and circumstances that wouldn't have been possible. He brings people into our lives that before we would have ignored or rejected. People around us are affected by His presence through us. We see this, because we believe, and it fuels the fire inside us.

**Within a few minutes, the room became a bedlam. It was the most absolute foolishness I have ever witnessed.**

Not long after Annette and I were born again, we were invited to dinner at the apartment of one of my co-workers. We were sitting around after dinner talking when one of the guests looked straight at Annette and asked, 'Have you just had a religious experience? You have the same look as one of my friends who says that she just met Jesus.' Annette's reply, of course, led immediately into a lengthy witness.

We hardly realized that as we were speaking, the hostess lit up a small pipe and began passing it around the circle of conversation. When it came to me, I just passed it along, without partaking, not aware of its contents or purpose. Within a few minutes, the room became a bedlam. It was the most absolute foolishness I have ever witnessed. People were facing each other, nose-to-nose, and both parties talking at the top of their voices. No one was listening to anyone else.

It was then, due to the odor of the smoke and the bizarre behavior of the participants, that we realized the contents of the pipe were 'hash'. Annette said to me, 'Pray in the Spirit.' We began praying, speaking out loud in other tongues. No one noticed; they probably thought we were high, too.

As fast as it started the bedlam subsided. The guests became very subdued. They came down off the high. The whole thing lasted only a few minutes, although I am told it would have usually lasted at least a half hour or longer. The people seemed sober and somewhat bewildered. They began to ask for their coats so that they could leave.

As time passes and such events seem to subside, we begin to cool off a bit. We get a little more studious and we begin to dig and look. We try to understand more with our minds, and that's not a bad thing, but a bit of the glow fades away. A year down the road we are beginning to get very serious. We are learning more of God's Word but it seems to be a bit more effort to walk the Christian walk than it was at first. The Scriptures don't come to us as easily as they used to. All our prayers are not immediately answered. God is preparing us to seek Him and causing us to grow.

As the years pass we tend to get mellow about our Christian walk. Indeed sometimes we get so mellow that the fire goes out almost altogether. I remember people telling me when I was first born again, 'Well you'll cool off!'

**As the years pass we tend to get mellow about our Christian walk.**

'No, not me, I'm not going to cool off.' I would always reply. But I found out they were right. I did cool off and I had to rekindle the fire.

## PRINCES

The other big problem is our reaction to people in the body. They become a problem when Christian leaders, for example, let us down by some unloving or unscriptural behavior. A Christian brother or sister may desert us when we need them. Our feelings get hurt for some reason or another. A saint, who once was close to us, reveals a confidence. The prayer line becomes a gossip line and loose talk cuts us like a knife. The church board gets into a political power struggle and we begin to see the frailties in the body that we love, the body we once thought was invincible. Psalm 146 tells us to 'Put not your trust in princes, in whom there is no help...' and to lean not on the 'son of man.' People are going to let us down. There is no flawless human, Christian or otherwise. Jesus was the only flawless person ever to walk the face of this earth. Someday, when I see Him face-to-face, I will be changed and be like him. Until that time I live in an earthen vessel that is perishing in a world that is corrupted and dying. The only solution is to follow the words of this song:

> Turn your eyes upon Jesus;
> Look full in His wonderful face,
>     and the things of earth
> Will grow strangely dim
> In the light of His glory and grace.

Paul tells us in Romans 12:11 that we must have fervor in our necessary service and avoid the lethargy that might otherwise settle in on us. In Acts 18:25 Apollo is described as being 'fervent in the Spirit, speaking and teaching the things of the Lord.' One of the ways in which we avoid lethargy is to diligently study and review the things of the Lord. What was Jesus like? What did Jesus do? What did Jesus say? If we speak what Jesus did, rather than what we or our church is doing we avoid self promotion. When we start talking about Jesus, avoid the complicated.   Just talking about Jesus, we get fervent in the Spirit. The glow increases and the flames start to leap.

## MYTHS

I love to debunk the myths that are taught in some of our churches. Recently someone came to me and said, 'All Christians are pacifists aren't they?' I'm not knocking pacifism but Jesus did not demonstrate such a position, and it's not in the Bible. Jesus had a lot to say about brotherly relationships, how we are to deal with each other, forgiveness and what you do with anger, but He never once advocated pacifism. Someone said to me, 'It's not good to have weapons, is it?' They were trying to put me on the spot because I am a hunter. My answer was, 'Gee, I don't know. Jesus told His disciples, 'He that hath no sword, let him sell his garment and, buy one.' And when they said, 'Here are two swords,' Jesus said that it was enough (Luke 22; 36, 38). Certainly no great spiritual lesson can be learned from this, but there are a lot of false conceptions that we can debunk when we know the words Jesus said.

## BLESSED HOPE

The life of Jesus in us rekindles the fire within us. Jesus exerts an influence on us by the life He lives. If we will but recall Jesus' life then and now, and speak those things Jesus did and what He is saying to you now, then there is confidence through the life of Jesus.

Paul says there is to be a hope in us and that we are to rejoice in it. WHAT IS YOUR HOPE TODAY, IN JESUS?

I think if I went around to Christian churches and I asked the members, 'What is your hope?' I'm sure that some of the answers would not be scripturally sound. DO YOU HAVE HOPE IN JESUS? You may say, 'Well, I'm saved.' Saved from what? For what? I remember the first time somebody asked me that question. I grew angry. I said, 'I met Jesus and you're trying to get me all involved in theology.' I should have been able to answer the man correctly, but I was new in the Lord so I didn't know how. I thought he was trying to trick me and maybe he was.

There are things we should know about the 'from whats' and 'for whats' of HOPE. Our hope is to see Him in glory and to join Him there. Our 'blessed hope' is the fact that we do not have to suffer judgment because we are His. He will stand in the way of judgment and release us and restore us to Himself and to the Father. That is a certain hope. It is certain according to the Scriptures. There is no hell fire in my future and I am not required to pay for my past life because I belong to the Lord Jesus and my name is written in the Lamb's Book of Life.

Romans chapter five lists some of the things in which we have our hope:

1) Peace
2) The hope of glory
3) Patience
4) Experience
5) Not being ashamed
6) Love
7) Atonement
8) Justification
9) Saved from wrath

These nine things are contained in the "blessed hope" that **we have in the Lord Jesus Christ**.

## ABEL, A MAN OF FAITH

In Hebrews 11 the great men of faith are reviewed as examples for us. Some of these may seem to be unlikely candidates at a cursory glance. For instance, Abel is mentioned as having offered an excellent sacrifice by FAITH (verse 4). I didn't realize that he did it by faith. I didn't see that the simple act of putting a lamb on the altar was such a great act of faith. Nonetheless, every time we give to God we do so by faith. If we give God an imperfect sacrifice, it is not done in faith and this is displeasing to God. When we offer a perfect sacrifice, it is acceptable unto God and, therefore, it is done in faith (see Rom 12:1). "Without faith it is impossible to please Him (God)" (Heb. 11:6), and "whatsoever is not of faith is sin" (Rom 14:23). "...He who comes to God (with an offering- a good sacrificial tithe or offering) must believe that He is (that He exists) and that He is a rewarder of all who diligently seek Him." (Hebrews 11:6)

Putting more than ten percent in the basket is often a difficult sacrifice. To do so means that we have to trust God to meet our unmet needs. However, Abel's act of taking a lamb out of his flock and putting it on the altar seems like only a ritual and not an act of great faith. The Scriptures say that Abel did it by faith and, because it was of faith, God witnessed to his righteousness. Now, Abel was the righteous brother, but what happened to Abel? He was murdered. Scripture says that his blood cried from the ground. When I first read that, I thought it meant that his blood cried for vengeance. However, it says that he speaks faith. "By it (faith) he, being dead, yet speaks." Abel did the right thing. He took care of his obligations. He was '**fervent in spirit; serving the Lord**.' By faith, he was rejoicing in something of the future that he could not yet see, not knowing that in a short time he would be a dead man. Yet because of the faith in what he did, he speaks to us from the grave. . This idea may 'mess' with, your theology if you are of the opinion that nothing bad ever happens to a 'man of faith.' Sometimes very difficult things do happen.

## JOSEPH

Another of the *Great Men of Faith* mentioned here in (verse 22) is Joseph. Joseph had faith and he gave a commandment concerning his bones. That's a funny thing to have faith about, isn't it? Joseph was responsible for bringing the Israelites into Egypt in the first place. You could be very cynical about it and say that Joseph and the Israelites were set up.

First of all, he was set up by getting the coat of many colors from his father. That coat became *the last straw* that caused his half brothers to be angry with him and to try to get rid of him. His father loved him more than the others because he was a child of his old age and a child of his favorite wife, Rachel. Even his birth order set him up. He had two prophetic dreams from God which contributed to his brothers' anger. They were so angry that they were ready to do him in entirely. Reuben's attempt to save Joseph's life ended in his being sold into slavery. If that wasn't bad enough, Joseph was placed in a household where he was so good that the Chief Guard of Pharaoh turned every thing over to him. The Chief Guard trusted Joseph so fully that he didn't even know what possessions he owned any more. Normally, that would be a very foolish position. For the Chief Guard's part, he should have managed his steward and made him accountable. For Joseph's part, he should have reported on a regular basis and kept his superior informed. Failure on either account makes both parties vulnerable.

We're all accountable to Jesus, aren't we? The problem with many people today is that they don't want to be accountable. They don't want to answer to anyone. They don't want to report to anybody. They think they want to be free, but they find that they fall into the worst kind of bondage in their struggle to be free.

Real freedom comes when you know the boundaries and you have a referee to keep you within them. In the church we find people who don't want anyone checking up on them. They resent the pastor doing his job by keeping the sheep in line. The pastor has a responsibility to keep a check on the spiritual condition of his charges since he is responsible for their souls. He will have to give an account to Jesus for what his people do and don't do.

For pastors that could be frightening. Why would anyone want to be a pastor and be placed in that kind of jeopardy? The nature of people is to be rebellious, but God says the pastor is accountable for you. Therefore, you are accountable to the pastor, like it or not. As long as you stay under that pastor's spiritual authority, he has to try to make the relationship work.

**Real freedom comes when you know the boundaries and you have a referee to keep you within them.**

In Joseph's case, however, he was not accountable to anybody because the Captain of the Guard had chosen to trust him so fully that he was virtually ignored. In Joseph's vulnerable position, he didn't realize that he had become vulnerable in other areas as well.

If Satan can find an opening, a chink in your armor, so to speak, he will manage to drive a dart through somehow. As I see it, Joseph was so honest that Satan could not use greed or mismanagement against him. Satan turned to Potiphar's wife and used her lust for him against Joseph. Joseph knew that he was in trouble with Potiphar's wife. Her advances went on day after day. He knew that she wanted him. She pestered him, but he did nothing about it. As time went on, he got a little careless. He allowed himself to be in the house with just himself and her. He put himself in the place of vulnerability. The Bible warns us to 'abstain from all appearance of evil (1 Thess. 5:22). Joseph was a white knight; he was such a good guy that it was unreal. Potiphar's wife said; 'Here I am, take me.'

Joseph replied, 'I cannot do that. I cannot betray the trust that your husband, Potiphar, has placed in me.' Well, you know the old saying, 'Hell hath no fury like that of a woman scorned.' It is not just true of women. Anybody who is scorned is likely to be furious. She grabbed Joseph's garment and pulled it off his body. He fled, presumably naked, out of the house. Then she made up lies about him.

Watch it, Christian! You dare not put yourself in the place of compromise and expect to escape unscathed. This is true whether you go into a bar or attend an R-rated movie, or whatever. You will not come out unscathed. If you place yourself in the path of temptation your reputation will be damaged. You will know that you have compromised and so will God, even if nobody else finds out, but they probably will. Flee from even the appearance of evil. Don't allow yourself to be put in that position where someone can say something that will damage your reputation. You will suffer for it for years. In the very rare instance you are compromised in the course of ministry by no fault or foolishness of yours, you can rely on God alone to provide the necessary covering and justification. In any case, you will never be able to defend yourself, so don't even try.

It appears that Joseph should not have been there but he was. As a result of his own righteousness he ended up in prison. Set up again! He was in prison for thirteen years. Upon his release, he was probably close to thirty years old. Again we see another set-up in the making. Sometime around the twelfth year, or before, I would have been as discouraged as our Frog Number One. But if we know any thing about Joseph, we recognize that he maintained his position with God. He was a prophetic man. He understood the prophetic visions of God. Yet even in prison his character was recognized and he was put in charge of all the prisoners. Two men from Pharaoh's house were placed in prison. They were the baker and the butler. These two men were assigned to Joseph. He was their servant and his job was to care for them while they were under arrest.

Both of the men had dreams which Joseph interpreted. Joseph prophesied that the baker would be killed while the butler would be restored to his position. Joseph told the butler to remember him and mention him to Pharaoh as he was in prison for no wrongdoing of his own.

As time went on the butler forgot Joseph. The butler was restored and two years passed before he had cause to remember. He remembered Joseph when Pharaoh had a dream that no one could analyze. It was then that the butler remembered the man in prison who had interpreted his dream. Joseph was summoned to Pharaoh and interpreted the ruler's dream along with **giving a solution to the problem it presented**. Joseph was able to draw on his experience as Potiphar's steward to formulate a plan. As a result, Pharaoh promoted Joseph, and made him the number two authority in the land. Joseph was elevated from prisoner to number two ruler, because God gave him **a miraculous interpretation**. No skill, no professional credentials, no resume of experience. Through the power of God he had been instantly raised to power. After twelve to fourteen years of being misused, misunderstood, imprisoned, lied about, and falsely accused, he was exalted to a position of authority and responsibility. Remember those prophetic dreams he had as a youth? Those dreams got him into trouble with his brothers; those dreams which his brothers tried to thwart. Not only did his brothers eventually come and bow down before him, but even his father did. Desiring to do good for his family, to supply their needs during the time of famine, he drew his family into Egypt. When he died, Joseph was 110 years old; he gave specific orders for the removal of his bones when the people left to possess the Promised Land. That is the testimony of a *Great Man of Faith.*

## RAHAB

There is one other person from the Bible whom I would like to bring to your attention. Hebrews 11:31 tells us that Rahab was not killed because of her faith... There is much written about Rahab in the Scriptures and Jewish rabbinical legend. She is spoken of by the rabbis as the most beautiful woman who ever lived. Men trembled when they saw her.

In spite of this power, Rahab was scared. She had heard about the Israelites how they had come out of Egypt, how they had journeyed through the wilderness; how they had been kept by God; how God had fed them from His hand; how they had marched over everyone who had tried to block their path.

Rahab told the Hebrew spies in Jericho that the people were frightened of Israel and their God. Jericho was thought to be a great invincible city with walls that were designed to fall outward on an attacking force. The people of Jericho were terrified, shaking in their boots when they heard about the approaching Israelites. The Israelites crossed the Jordan and they came on because Rahab received their spies and took them into her house of ill repute. They would not have normally gone there, in a thousand years since they believed it would have made them unclean, but they went in as God led them.

She received them, hid them, and even lied for them. A lying harlot became a helper of the men of Israel. She told them to give a sign to place in her window so that she and her family would not perish when everyone else did. They gave her a single red thread to tie in her window. If she did not do so she would be killed, but if she tied the thread as they directed her to do, she would be saved. We are told that her home was in the Wall of Jericho, built right into those walls that were supposed to fall outward on the attackers. This was not unusual in that many of the homes were built into the walls of cities. Rahab and her family were to stay inside during the attack. The archeologists now say that the walls did indeed fall, but they fell inward. I saw these walls and could see how they fell. Virtually the entire wall fell, but we know that one part didn't fall. Rahab and her family were safe inside that part of the wall. Not only were they saved by a miracle, but they were saved by a miracle within a miracle. Walls, which were super strong and designed to fall outward, fell spontaneously inward - all except Rehab's house. This passage of scripture tells me, that a frightened harlot, who betrayed her people and lied her way into safety, received those Israelite spies by faith. Condemned by her own people who were about to die at the hands of an invading army, she received them by faith. Bill Johnson says in his book <u>Secrets To Imitating God</u> that it was because she heard that the Hebrew God protected them. That was a different kind of god than any she had heard about. Rahab went on to become the mother of Boaz, the kinsman—redeemer, a prototype of Christ. Boaz and his wife, Ruth, the Moabitess, and Rahab, the harlot, are all in the lineage of Jesus.

## <u>HOLD ON</u>

These Old Testament saints, though dead, are yet alive. "So then we are surrounded by such a great cloud of witnesses..." (Hebrews 12:1). Their testimony of faith, believing God for what had not yet come to be seen, speaks to us down through history. Through impossible situations they held on to see the day of salvation.

Let us not allow sloppiness to spoil our work. We must keep the flame of the Spirit burning as we do our work for the Lord. Our job is to build our happiness on our hope in Christ. When trials come, and they will, we must endure them patiently. It is our responsibility to build a lifestyle of prayer and steadfastly maintain it (Rom.12:11-12, paraphrased).

ARE YOU LIVING A LIFESTYLE OF PRAYER?
If not, it's urgent to reset your priorities and begin anew.

## <u>Pray with me.</u>

Father, forgive me for the lack of prayer in my life. By Your Spirit infuse new life in me and help me in my own weakness to restructure my day to include communication with you. AMEN

*Robert and Annette – Christmas 2008*

*Robert with daughter, Jenn, and grandchildren,*
*Hunter and Madysen, Christmas 2009*

# CHAPTER NINE

## Seeds Of Hospitality Grow Fruit

### THERE WAS AN OLD LADY WHO LIVED IN A...

I fought the sound of the alarm clock. I didn't want to get up. As I shook the blanket of sleep from my brain, I realized that my wife was sitting on the side of the bed in anguish. It was dark out and the clock showed only 1 a.m. It was not the alarm that had awakened me but Annette's crying out. Her pain was intense. I tried to overcome our fear and extend faith to her, praying against this attack. 'God's man of faith and power' didn't have it that night, however.

I drove to the hospital, trying not to hit any bumps to jar her, yet moving as fast as possible. After what seemed an interminable wait in the emergency room, and many examinations later, the culprit was diagnosed. Peritonitis made the necessity for an immediate operation obvious to the doctors. My wife and I prayed and kissed and before long, they took her to surgery. Afterwards, they brought Annette into her room. It was then I noticed the small frame of the person in the bed next to hers. After eight long hours, I went home to grab some recovery sleep.

Our mutual **recoveries** went swiftly. By the time I got back to her room, Annette had already been up and walking. Something else had taken place as well. She had met the lady in the next bed. It was the beginning of a strange one way love relationship. The wrinkled old lady in the next bed was the most unlovable person you could imagine. She was abrupt and rude. She was caked with the years of unwashed dirt. An odor hung about her that spoke of unruly cats. Yet both Annette and I were somehow drawn to her.

Over the next few months, we visited Helen at her house. It was a run down half of a duplex in a less-than-savory part of town. She would never let us in the house. She gave many different excuses. But always there was that horrible odor. Her ever-present dogs and cats obviously contributed to the stench. Flies and other insects hovered everywhere. Recently widowed, Helen had no relatives, and no real friends, only drinking buddies. She liked to go up to the corner bar for just one beer. Well, maybe just one.

Once, when we discovered it was her birthday, we invited her to come to our house. Annette even managed to get her into the tub and she washed Helen's hair. Clean clothes, along with newly coiffed and scrubbed hair, did not succeed in making her into a new person, however. We had a cookout that day, and a birthday cake. It was the first birthday party Helen had ever had. She was now eighty. Her tears told us how much she appreciated the occasion.

We got to know her and to be known as Helen's 'rich friends from the suburbs.' We surely weren't rich, but I guess we were by comparison. Neighbors began to reveal some facts that Helen had kept well hidden. Winter was coming and the oil man would not deliver any heating fuel because of the stench. Helen did not have a flushable toilet so she used a pail. She would dump the contents in the toilet, followed by a bucket of water. There was no hot water and no working refrigerator in her home. She slept in a downstairs front room, and had not been upstairs for sometime. My fourteen-year-old son Emory and I cleaned up the back yard of her house, loading the pickup truck, twice, filling it with garbage, junk, and dog feces so that an oil delivery could be made. In the process we began to discover far more than we bargained for.

Helen finally let me in the front door. I stared with shock and disbelief. The only thing I could compare it to was the garbage dump where I hunted rats as a kid. You could find every kind of waste in her living room. I couldn't even open the front door more than just enough to barely squeeze through. Once I got in, there was hardly a place to stand. The bed in a far corner was the only clear place and several dogs of suspect origin and health were resting there. There were unwashed empty cat food cans and dirty dishes piled higher than my head. How could she have lived in such a manner?

After a full Saturday's work and three truckloads, I could not even guess how much was left to do. I began to realize that it was more than I could handle. For the next several weeks we negotiated the red tape of the city agencies. We managed to get temporary care for Helen. They cleaned, fumigated, and repaired. It wasn't any palace but it was at least sanitary.

The lady from the city agency who cared for Helen befriended her. I wish that I could tell you some great outcome, but 'eighty-year-old tigers' aren't likely to change their stripes. She once told us that she had accepted Christ, but then she told us a lot of things.

## FOUNDATIONS

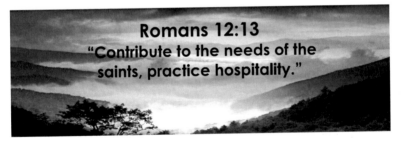

**Romans 12:13**
"Contribute to the needs of the saints, practice hospitality."

**James 1:27** "Religion that is pure and undefiled before God and the Father is this: to visit orphans and widows in their affliction, and to keep oneself unstained from the world."

# FORMULA FOR SUCCESS

Matthew Benjamin Stagmer was born on December 10, 1982. That was the first year of our new ministry- a church and a twelve grade school with kindergarten.

When Matt was born I was deeply involved in developing the new ministry. Annette had had a difficult pregnancy and at age forty she was slow to regain her former energy. We were struggling. Spiritually, there seemed to be battles to be fought on every plane. None of our enemies wanted us to succeed. As we were to find out later, our most dangerous adversaries were within. Physically, I was dog-tired and Annette had been drained by the demands of the pregnancy and the new baby. Financially, we were on the rocks. I had spent every penny I had to get the ministry up and running. The new ministry was on shaky financial ground to begin with and in order to compensate, I was not receiving any salary. Simply put, we were broke.

Matthew was a child of promise to us. Seven years before he was born, Annette was told by the Lord that she would have a son whose name would be Matthew Benjamin. At the time, the doctors said it would be impossible for her to conceive a child. A lovely daughter, Jennifer, and a miscarriage intervened during those seven years.

It seems that from his birth Matt's life was in danger. Early, he developed an allergy to cow's milk and had to have special formula. The additional financial burden broke the family bank. In addition he had a rare bronchial condition and would suddenly awake unable to breathe, sounding like the barking like a dog. We held tightly to those prophetic statements that had told us that Matthew would be his father's right-hand helper. Matthew means 'gift of God' and Benjamin means 'son of the right hand.'

A group of African-American Christians from an inner-city church that had recently become involved in our school became aware of our need. They sent us a supply of the precious formula. They continued to supply us with formula for the rest of that year. We really appreciated that wonderful gift in our time of need.

Sometime later we attended a church dinner with those saints. Although I had some idea of their situation, neither Annette nor I was prepared for the hardship condition that those faithful ones experienced regularly. Our situation paled in comparison to theirs. Actually, there was no comparison.

Although their building was large, it seemed to be in need of every kind of repair. They sat on an assortment of mismatched pews and chairs. The floor covering ran from bare wood to threadbare carpet to tattered linoleum. The walls were covered with several unmatched colors of paint.

The worship in that place was joyful and sincere. Let it simply be said that these people really understood sacrifice and the meaning of agape love. Their 'widow's mite' offering, which meant life for my child, was beyond value in heavenly eyes.

**Their 'widow's mite' offering, which meant life for my child, was beyond value in heavenly eyes.**

Six years passed and I was told about a wonderful thing that happened to those dear people. A large suburban church of a different denomination, without strings attached, had performed a wide-scale and costly renovation on their building. The faithful band of followers now had a very nice facility. But that's not all. That large church has undertaken an evangelism program in that neighborhood of the city. Where do you think they sent the fruit of their labors? Not to the suburbs, but to my friends in their transformed facility.

The seeds that those Christians planted, unselfishly, have returned abundant fruit into their bosom.

How do you see yourself contributing to those in need?
Do you sow seeds of hospitality?
What is your involvement in pure and undefiled religion?

# CHAPTER TEN

# Blessing And Cursing

## KEEPING THE FEAST.

"Why is this night different than all other nights?" The annually repeated question seemingly goes unanswered. The father recites God's faithfulness through the history of the Jewish people. Passover, with its solemn recitations and joyful feasting, has begun. The Father takes the three pieces of matzah wrapped in a napkin and breaking two of the three pieces, he wraps up the third. A young son playfully hides the wrapped pièce of matzah under a pillow. It will be retrieved at the end of the meal. Only unleavened bread will be eaten at this meal, and throughout the succeeding week.

A great deal of preparation has already been made. For a full week the ladies have cleaned every nook and cranny of the home. Not a crumb of leaven may remain. Pots and pans, dishes and cups, are washed and rewashed. Not satisfied, but exhausted, the cleaning finally comes to a halt. In the strictest of households a Rabbi is invited to examine the residence and proclaim it ceremonially clean. Should the inspector find even the smallest crumb, the whole process must be repeated. Now the food preparation begins.

Today, as in past times and where possible, a lamb is selected. It must be a perfect lamb without blemish and it becomes a member of the household. More precious than a domestic pet, the adorable wooly baby is cuddled, loved and pampered. For at least four days, but in many cases for much longer, the lamb is part of the family. Then ceremonially, its feet are tied. The throat is slit by a rabbi with the sharpest of knives. Each heart of the family members is seized by the costly sacrifice. The family mourns as its lost member is prepared for the feast. Such is the bitter sweetness of Passover.

## FOUNDATION

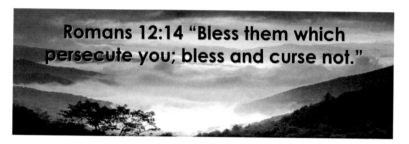

Romans 12:14 "Bless them which persecute you; bless and curse not."

**I Corinthians 5:7-8** "Purge out, therefore, the old leaven that ye may be a new lump, as ye are unleavened. For even Christ our Passover is sacrificed for us. Therefore let us keep the feast, **not with old leaven, neither with the leaven of malice and wickedness**; but with the unleavened bread of sincerity and truth."

**Exodus 12:15** "Seven days shall ye eat unleavened bread; even the first day **ye shall put away leaven out of your houses**: for whosoever eateth leavened bread from the first day until the seventh day, that soul shall be CUT OFF from Israel."

## ENOUGH TO EAT

The hungry multitude on the hillside was reluctant to go scavenging. The ministry was sweet and intense. The disciples sensed the pulling in opposite directions. Coming to the Master, they broached the problem with Him. They suggested that it was time to end the ministry and send the 5,000 away. Jesus said, "They need not depart; give ye them to eat." The men looked at their meager larder and the teeming multitude. Dismayed, they exclaimed that they had only five loaves and two fishes. Never the less, Jesus told them to bring it. You know the story, how He blessed it, and gave it for distribution. The food never ran out. There even was considerable excess left over. It was a miracle! Jesus caused the bread and fish to multiply simply **by a blessing**.

Sometime after they departed to the other side of the Sea of Tiberius, they realized they had no bread. Jesus used the opportunity to complete the lesson. To the multitude, the miracle was just that, a miracle. To the disciples, however, it was to become **an object lesson on faith**. "Beware of the leaven of the Pharisees..." Numbed by needs of the flesh, the disciples thought only of food. Jesus upbraided them for their failure to see beyond the obvious.

**Matthew 16:11-12** (NIV) "How is it you don't understand that I was not talking to you about bread? But be on your guard against the yeast of the Pharisees and Sadducees. [12]Then they understood that he was not telling them to guard against the yeast used in bread, but against the teaching of the Pharisees and Sadducees" He spoke of malice, wickedness, and hypocrisy of the hearts of the Pharisees and the Sadducees which underlay an outward show of religion which really perverted the Law. They called down curses on themselves and others by their self-righteous condemnation. Jesus refreshed the minds of His followers by recalling the miracle of loaves. The loaves were multiplied beyond even the needs of the moment. How had it occurred?

**"ALL SIN HAS CORPORATE CONSEQUENCES. There are no private sins.**

### BREAD OF LIFE

Unaware that it would be their last meal together, the disciples shared the Passover meal. In the midst of the meal, Jesus took the bread- the unleavened bread. He <u>blessed it and broke it</u> and then declared, "This is my body..." **Jesus was the unleavened bread.** Jesus was without sin.

## BAKING BREAD

The baker carefully sifts flour and salt together. Yeast is placed in a separate bowl; warm water is added. The yeast begins to form brownish foam. After a brief wait the yeast is mixed with the flour to which salt, eggs, and shortening have already been added. The baker kneads the mixture then places it in a warm place. In forty-five minutes to one hour the mixture has doubled in volume due to the yeast raising the mix. The cook punches and flattens the mixture. Again he must wait. Once again the mixture doubles. More punching, more waiting, formed into loaves, it again rests. Then it is placed into the oven. The tantalizing odor of freshly baked bread fills the kitchen.

Jesus likened yeast to sin. Its properties are similar. A little leaven permeates the whole mixture. Sin, however disguised, contaminates all that it contacts. My axiom is **"ALL SIN HAS CORPORATE CONSEQUENCES."** There are no private sins. That is a lie that has been told so often that most people believe it. But in an immoral atmosphere all society is affected. Leaven expands by producing gas. Sin puffs up and produces false confidence. You cannot hide sin because it gets bigger. It starts in the mind and affects the whole body. The Pharisees were depending on unrighteous mammon to make them great. Jesus demonstrated that to be great one must stay small. Leaven serves only to puff one up.

## SOME SICK, SOME SLEEP

How do you come to the communion table? Do you come with leaven in your life? Get the leaven out. If you don't, you will eat and drink condemnation unto yourself. Consider the Body of Christ. Jesus was unleavened. When you come to the communion table you are the sacrifice being presented, Jesus has already been sacrificed. You are to be **"...a living sacrifice, holy acceptable unto God, which is your reasonable service."** Do you have something against a brother or does a brother have something against you? Go settle the matter of dispute first. Then come back to the table. Is there a besetting sin? Repent, ask forgiveness. <u>Get the leaven out</u>. It's too dangerous to eat and drink unworthily. Whoever should eat the feast with leaven, that household will be cut off from the house of Israel.

## A BOWL OF FRUIT BRINGS FRUIT.

I had been having an awful time with my boss. It wasn't that he was such a tyrant, but I just couldn't seem to get on his wave length. I was frustrated. Every time I thought I understood his instructions and began to do what I thought he wanted, it seemed that I did it the wrong way or that I did the wrong thing. It got to the point that I began giving him back his oral instructions in writing so that I was sure we understood each other. He took offense to that procedure as though I was trying to ensnare him in something. Even with the orders in writing, it seemed to me that he constantly changed direction so that I couldn't win.

I came home and griped to my wife. I didn't have anyone else to talk to about it. She, of course, took my side. In her sympathy to me, Annette began to feel really bitter toward my boss. She felt as though I was being treated unfairly by my incompetent superior. I thought so too.

Within a few hours Annette began to complain about a stiffness and soreness in her hands. We had heard teachings that explained the connection between physical illness, and the harboring of bitterness. We knew that we had to deal with the bitterness that we were both experiencing.

We knew that the arthritis was a curse and that the opposite of a curse was a blessing. Scripture says that Job was restored when he prayed for his friends, who were also his detractors (Job 42:10). So, in order to break the curse we began to pray blessing on the boss and his family.

Prayer alone did not seem to be enough. God impressed on Annette that we needed to express our lack of bitterness in a more tangible manner. Annette thought of a way. She suggested that we invite the boss and his wife to dinner.

We were very hard pressed financially at the time, but we decided to pull out all the stops and make this the most festive occasion possible. Annette fixed a fabulous dinner of her specialty, chicken curry, with all the trimmings. In the center of the table, set with our finest china and cut glass goblets, was a very large cut-glass compote that had been handed down through my family. In the bowl was the most colorful mixed fruit salad. It was a feast set for a king.

The boss and his wife were overwhelmed. They couldn't get their eyes off of that expensive fruit compote. Dinner was delicious. The conversation was joyful, punctuated with laughter coming freely from all corners of the table. After dinner, we retired to the living room. Even the candles were lit. Deferring to the boss, I gave him the most comfortable chair. After a brief light conversation, the boss began to tell some very entertaining stories of his experiences. We all had a good time laughing and talking. The evening ended on a high note with every one sorry it had come to a close.

Did that change everything? Immediately, Annette's pain left and we weren't bitter any more. Things went somewhat better on the job and several months later my boss got a better job in another city.

## 5000 X 5 LOAVES PLUS 2 FISH = BLESSING

How did Jesus multiply the provision? He blessed it. He broke it. He gave it out. Blessing, He is blessing. Truth, He is truth. Increase, He is increase. No unrighteousness; no mammon; no leaven; no sin; He is blessing! It is Christ in you the hope of glory. **You bless and curse not**. After creating man God blessed them and said unto them, "Be fruitful, and multiply, and replenish the earth and subdue it and have dominion...."

# CLEAN OUT YOUR HOUSE. GET OUT THE LEAVEN.

Say, "I'm not having it!" At school, work, leisure, and at church watch your attitude, your thoughts, and your talk. Avoid all gossip, because gossip is sin. It is leaven and brings a curse. Bless and curse not. When someone hurts your feelings or says something false about you, pray a blessing on them. If there's someone you have trouble with, pray for his or her salvation and bless them. Say, "Bless her/him, Lord. Give her/him the best of new shoes, new clothing (even better than mine). Bless her/him with more friends than I have. Bless her/him, Lord. Give her/him a better job and a new car." Bless here, bless there. "Lord, show me how to interact with her/him and how to show forth your love."

**Be a blessing to them like Jesus is.**

God will give the increase, not hot air from leaven.

**Be sincere.**

Let the answers to your prayers be the substance of your own blessing.

**Be full of truth.**

Speak blessings and you will be lifted up.

*Robert and Annette at tax protest in Annapolis, Maryland*

# CHAPTER ELEVEN

# Mind Not

## FOUNDATIONS

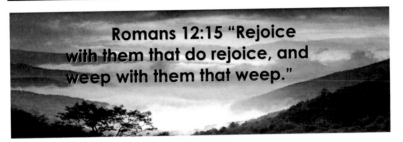

Romans 12:15 "Rejoice with them that do rejoice, and weep with them that weep."

## TOM'S NEW SONG

Since meeting Jesus, Tom had been transformed from a hard fighting, hard drinking cowboy to a marshmallow. What a sweet guy he had become. Tom was lanky and tanned, with premature graying of his temples; he was good-looking and fun to be with. After going through our Life in the Spirit Seminar, Tom decided to be a group discussion leader. His leadership potential was recognized so it wasn't long before he was asked to become a co-seminar leader. At each meeting of the eight-week seminar, the leader would introduce the topic with a short talk before the anxious groups would break into threes and fours for discussion. The first time Tom spoke, his topic was salvation. He never finished his second sentence. This handsome hulk of a guy, towering over the seated participants, just stood there and cried. You could barely understand a word he choked out over the sobs. I cried too. So did everyone else. I believe that people were transformed that night as Tom shed his bittersweet tears, unashamed. We all harmonized with his new song to the Lord.

## REJOICE OR WEEP

Rejoice! We all like to rejoice. When someone is happy, it's easy to be happy with them. Weep! Now that's something else again. If someone stands before you and begins to choke up as he speaks, you may be able to identify with him. Maybe he is in distress as he recalls a past situation. We can all feel those things. We may even get a little teary-eyed or start to choke up ourselves. We may start to bless God and pray for the person. That's not too difficult, that kind of weeping.

**Just how are we expected to see the hurt or the joy which _doesn't_ show?**

How about the person who is weeping on the inside, however? If I showed up on Sunday morning with my arm in a sling every one would be very solicitous toward me, I'm sure. "Oh, pastor, what happened?" "Well, I was trimming my apple tree and I fell off the ladder."

They would be very concerned. "Poor pastor, he hurt his arm."

You would be very careful not to bump into my arm. You would look for things to do to make it easier for me. But what about the times you don't see my hurt? If I wasn't wearing a sling or showing any signs like a cast; if I made no mention of it, if I wasn't showing any tears in the corner of my eyes, you would have a hard time identifying with the hurt in my arm. If I express my joy or my heart visibly and externally it's easy for you to pick up on it.

# SUPERNATURAL EYES

How do we get our minds attuned, without direct communication to what someone else in the body is going through? It has to be supernatural doesn't it?

Yesterday, for example, I met an old friend in the library. I had not seen her for at least six months. After we exchanged hugs, I told her that I had been seeing her every where.

I would turn a corner and there she would be. No, it wasn't her but someone who would remind me of her. After this happened several times, I finally got the message and began to pray in the spirit for her. As I related this to her I could sense that she was touched. She told me of several difficult medical tests that she was undergoing. The doctors suspected a serious illness. We both agreed that God had communicated her need to me so that I might pray with her through this difficult time. I wish that I was always so spiritually aware.

This takes a 'renewing of the mind.' Only the resurrected mind stays tuned to God. What's a resurrected mind? The only reference you could find in scripture would be to Jesus in the resurrected body. He wasn't immediately recognizable. Even though the disciples had been with Him constantly for three years they did not know Him at first. That's strange. You would think that at least one of them would have said, 'That guy looks like Jesus,' but they didn't. He did some things with His resurrected body that blows our minds. He appeared in a locked room. We don't know how he got in there. Did he walk through a wall? He didn't open the door.

# ENTROPY AND THE CHRISTIAN

The youthful science teacher in the Christian school spoke on a very technical subject. With my limited expertise I will attempt to condense the pertinent part of what he explained to his audience. His subject was <u>Entropy</u>. He said that disorder in the universe entered in through sin, and order in the universe enters in through Jesus Christ.

The fall of man caused disorder in the universe. Watchman Nee's book <u>The Latent Power of the Soul</u>, states the premise that man was created as a mentally and physically powerful being. That power was lost through the Fall. It has been restored through The Lord Jesus Christ. We *can* see that restoration in part in this life, but the fullness of it will take place when we see Jesus face-to-face. His Kingdom is a now Kingdom. Wherever Jesus rules is His Kingdom. As He is, so are we in this world. I think that as we walk in harmony with Him we are like Him in His kingdom. We will manifest powers such as being able to he transported without the aid of a vehicle, and to transcend barriers as He did in His resurrected body.

## THE MIND OF CHRIST OVER MATTER

It was a dreary night. The bus full of sleepy people was returning from an anti-abortion rally. The fog had become rather dense with intermittent rain. The streets were slick. Traffic was heavy. I was driving; feeling tired but managing to stay alert. Suddenly a large dump truck swerved in front of me, cutting the bus off and stopped dead in front of us. In a split second of eternity, I judged that the safest maneuver was to steer off to the right onto the shoulder. I could see the bridge abutment coming up. At worst I might brush it with the side of the bus. To hit the truck would have been certain death for me and several others. As I steered to the right the uneven road surface hidden from my view suddenly threw the vehicle to the right so that the right front wheel and fender were directly aligned with the abutment. I braced for the impact of the collision. Someone screamed. Another person hollered, "Jesus!" An eternity of silence preceded the crunch of steel on concrete. I watched in stunned amazement as the fender met the bridge and calmly passed through it.

Others watched too. There was no noise no jolt, and the bus passed the truck and I, still in a stupor, steered it off the shoulder onto the roadway safely. Yes, we hit that bridge. There is no way we could have avoided it. It was no illusion. There were other witnesses, including my wife, who will testify that we did hit that bridge. The bus hit the bridge and passed through it unharmed.

Experience says that such a thing can't happen. Two solid objects cannot pass through each other. Solid objects are very dense and hard. However, they are composed of moving molecules. These molecules move very slowly but they are moving.

Our bodies are made up of moving molecules. Think of an ice cube. The water molecules in that cube are moving. If we heat up that ice, the molecules move faster until the cube loses its shape and we have water in its liquid form. Keep heating it and the molecules move faster and faster until it becomes steam. We have not changed the molecules. It is still H20. We have altered its density. The ice is hard; the water is soft; the steam is without form. Steam is totally able to move through space and some other objects, depending upon their density. If then the density of two solid objects could be altered by kinetic process those solid objects could pass through each other without harm or alteration of their basic composition. Could this possibly happen to our bodies in a resurrected state? Could we then walk through a wall? We know that two solid objects cannot pass through each other, yet we saw it happen. Jesus did it for us.

> I live now in faith towards what I know will be. Thus I am able to overcome certain barriers by faith.

When I am transformed to be like Jesus, all the effects of sin will be passed away from me. Then my recomposed person will have unlimited potential. I will be able to transcend all barriers of time, space and density. I live now in faith towards what I know will be. Thus I am able to overcome certain barriers by faith. Though I must wait to claim my resurrected body, the Scriptures tell me that I can get a resurrected mind in this life. A resurrected mind is the mind of Christ, a mind that is not restricted by time, space or density. Such a mind can conceive of things **which are not** and **create them into existence**. Such a mind is attuned to the promptings of The Holy Spirit. Such a mind can be of the same mind one toward another. If our mind is renewed as one day our bodies will be, then we have a new thought process. Fed and gifted by the Holy Spirit, we have 'word gifts' - prophecy, interpretation, words of knowledge, understanding, Hallelujah! A mind that has not been renewed cannot get those things, it cannot even conceive of it. The renewed mind can function in the spirit with discernment. I can know what your needs are and what you are going through. I can be like minded with you in the spirit.

Spiritual things are spiritually discerned. We can weep with you when you are weeping, although in the physical we see nothing. We may not be able to see anything, but we are able to rejoice with you even though we don't see you rejoicing.

The Body of Christ has not yet arrived at having such a mature renewed mind. You can see the potential and we can even understand that it is what God means it to be. So how do we get there? The answer is that through **renewing our minds** we are transformed individually and collectively. We bring our minds, thoughts, and actions into alignment with the moment by moment presence of Holy Spirit and the Living Word.

# CHAPTER TWELVE

# Wise Versus Wisdom

## FOUNDATIONS

> **Romans 12:16**
> Be of the same mind one toward another. Mind not high things, but condescend to men of low estate. Be not wise in your own conceits.

## HIGH CLASS OR LOW CLASS CHRISTIANS?

Jesus demonstrated a classless caring for people. It takes a lot of changing for most of us to transcend our social-class level. When revival broke out at the large, impersonal church I once attended and the Holy Spirit took charge of people's lives it was not at all strange to see a dirty teenager, in blue jeans, next to a wealthy dowager in mink. Ten years later, when the fire of revival had dwindled, the faces seem to look more and more alike. The social concerns are still there but the personal involvement is nil. Condescending to men of low estate does not mean that we climb down off the perch to get our hands dirty for a while. Rather, it means that our minds get attuned with God so that we are able to discern the needs of others. In the spirit I can touch people if I am not bound by my own conceit.

## HARRY'S FIRE

Harry stood in the pulpit. The emotion in his voice was a mirror reflection of his heart. Harry loved the Lord and defiantly proclaimed His Word to the sober, almost angry congregation. They didn't like that kind of preaching. After a year and six months with numerous converts to Christ, Harry was transferred to a church thirty miles away. He wasn't disappointed. As far as I know, he's still winning the lost to Jesus. He hadn't always been so brave.

When I met Harry he was preaching a sloppy mixture of platitudes and vague promises. When he had first come to that cold denominational church he had been full of vigor. His hell-fire-and-damnation sermons, punctuated with altar calls, had not lasted long. The powerbrokers of that group's inner circle simply told him to stop it or he would be removed. The governing body of this congregation was laced with Freemasons. My grandfather and father were Freemasons and they were on the board of our family's home church! **Freemasonry** and biblical Christianity <u>do not mix</u>. The Freemasons have their own Bible and their own set of beliefs. At first glance it looks the same, but in the New Testament parts of certain verses have been omitted. For example, "...**No man comes to the father but by me**." (Jesus ) <u>is omitted.</u> +

**Here we let Freemasonry speak for itself:**
**"Freemasonry is not Christianity ... it admits men of every creed within its hospitable bosom...."An Encyclopedia of Freemasonry, by Albert G. Mackey, 1921, pp. 618-619.**

**Freemasonry says they know the secret name of God. Freemasonry's god is a triune deity called JoaBulOn which stands for Jehovah, Baal, and Osiris.**

The following report compares and contrasts Freemasonry and Christianity:

**From: Christ or the Lodge? A Presbyterian Report on Freemasonry, a report presented at the ninth General Assembly of the Orthodox Presbyterian Church, meeting at Rochester, New York, June 2–5, 1942,**

- Christianity lays claim to the only true God, the God of the Bible, and denounces all other Gods as idols. Masonry recognizes the Gods of all religions.

- Christianity describes God as the Father of Jesus Christ and of those who through faith in Him have received the right to be called the sons of God. The God of Masonry is the universal father of all mankind.

- Christianity holds that only the worship of the God who has revealed Himself in Holy Scripture is true worship. Masonry honors as true worship the worship of numerous other deities.

- Christianity recognizes but one Savior, Jesus Christ, the only Mediator between God and man. Masonry recognizes many saviors.

- Christianity acknowledges but one way of salvation, that of grace through faith. Masonry rejects this way and substitutes for it salvation by works and character.

- Christianity teaches the brotherhood of those who believe in Christ, the communion of saints, the church universal, the one body of Christ. Masonry teaches the brotherhood of Masons and the universal brotherhood of man.

- Christianity glories in being the one truly universal religion. Masonry would rob Christianity of this glory and appropriate it to itself.

- Christianity maintains that it is the only true religion. Masonry denies this claim and boasts of being Religion itself.

Freemasonry is not compatible with the Gospel of the Kingdom that Jesus preached. Freemasons are known for their trying to do good works. However good these works are they do not lead to or reflect salvation in the name of Jesus. When asked if they did not do good works Jesus said, "… away from me. I never knew you." (Matthew 7:22)

Removal spells death to the career of a denominational preacher. So Harry toned it down and down and down, until there was no more glow at all. For two years he preached like that. The congregation was happy. The bishop was happy. Harry was being talked about as a future district superintendent. He even began to believe he was doing a good job. But, inside, Harry wasn't happy. More than any thing else, Harry knew that his own prayer and worship were virtually extinct. Despite his attempts, God was just too distant. Besides, the needs of the people in this large congregation were pressing in on him. He spent many hours in his office and study trying to deal with the administrative details, studying to placate his sophisticated listeners. Then there were the endless committee meetings, numerous house calls, hospital visits, and counseling sessions. Harry even had an assistant but that involved staff meetings and scheduling. His wife had her share of ministry responsibilities as well as caring for the children and keeping the house in a state of perfection. All ministers live in a gold fish-bowl environment. Success! The money was good. His reputation flourished.

But Harry wasn't happy. The cracks in the facade began to show. He experienced family problems, church unrest, community requests and complaints, and the ever-present political power struggle among the church board. Then something strange happened.

As Harry looked out on the sober faces on Sunday morning, two people actually smiled at him. No, it was not just a pleasant, friendly smile; many people smiled that way. This smile was different. It was encouraging. His eyes were drawn to the faces of those two smiling people. They listened intently, nodding agreement when the Scriptures were proclaimed. They prayed intensely, their lips moving slightly as the morning prayers were read. They seemed to rejoice openly when the choir sang its polished-to-perfection anthem. At sermon time they took out Bibles and pencils.

How long had it been since he had seen someone open a Bible in church? During the sermon one of them actually mouthed a silent amen. At offering time, as the Doxology was played, the other one raised both hands, extending them straight in the air. This was too much!

Harry took his customary greeting spot at the back of the church. His mind wasn't on the "Hello. How are you?" "Thank you very much." "That's nice." or "I didn't know that," kind of niceties. He was looking for those shining faces he had seen in the congregation. Before long they were in front of him. He blurted out his prepared request, "May I see you in my study in a few minutes?"

"Why, yes," said the gentleman. He was wearing a tweed coat, which by its cut, was obviously expensive. His face was more interesting than handsome. Harry guessed that the man was in his mid thirties. The answer was at once a relief and a new sort of trauma. What would he say? Why had he asked them to meet him? He continued to perform the required amenities, while his mind was preoccupied with the upcoming meeting. The eternal line of well-wishers slowly diminished, and then finally the last was gone.

Harry negotiated the stairs without looking, his long black preacher's robe flowing behind him. Standing before the seated pair, his eloquence gone, he said only, "Wha— what happened? "

The stylish, yet dignified, pair looked quizzically at each other and then smiled. Harry knew the answer before it was spoken. He knew it the first moment he had made eye contact with them in the sanctuary. He just wanted to hear them say it. "We have met Jesus," was the inevitable reply.

"Tell me about it, the pastor requested. Again they held a conference with their eyes. With the silent assent of her partner, the lady began. Harry noted that she simply glowed with a freshness that believers possess when they begin to speak about meeting their Lord.

"I'm a teacher. I teach elementary children in the inner city. We had been married only a few weeks and were very happy. I thought that I really had it made. My goals in life seemed to be really coming together. But when I was alone, I just couldn't stop crying. I didn't know why - fear I suppose - that I would lose everything. Then one night, as I was crying, I heard, "Jesus is the Rock of All Ages." I cried out to God, "Are you really alive doing the same things you did when you were living on earth?" It was about a week later when a close friend came by. She began to tell me about her sister, whom I had previously met. Her sister, a minister's wife, had elephantitis. She had received treatments by several doctors but nothing helped. Then she went to small group Bible study, was prayed for, and miraculously healed. She showed me before and after pictures. It was truly amazing my friend insisted that Jesus had healed her sister...."

She continued to speak for about twenty minutes. When it was over, Harry's hot tears flowed down his cheeks. He expressed his joy, thanked the couple and invited them to pray with him. Once again his preacher's prepared eloquence failed. After a brief opening, he fell silent and the woman took up the slack. Her prayer was rich in praise and thanksgiving, much like a personal prayer to a close friend. Harry felt that warmth inside that he had missed so long. Then they both placed their hands on his shoulders and began speaking a lovely language he did not recognize. He could feel an electrifying heat through his robe and his shirt where their hands lightly touched him. Time was suspended.

When the prayer was over, it was difficult to return to the present.

The change in Harry was dramatic. Now there was time to pray. Worship again became his number one priority. The Bible became the most used book, in his study once more, but now Harry was reading for himself rather than for something to preach. As he prayed for his staff they seemed to do a better job, leaving him more time for his priorities. Little by little the fire returned to the pulpit.

> Worship again became his number one priority. The Bible became the most used book in his study once more, but now Harry was reading for himself rather than for something to preach.

This story ends well. All too often stories like this end in heartbreak for the minister or those to whom ministry has been given. I meet people everywhere who once were strong Christians, even leaders, who have fallen away. There is a hidden crisis in Christianity today. Why the injury? Why are individuals who are capable of dynamic leadership sitting in the back pews of large

> Therefore, we have on the one hand, the positive attributes of ambition and self esteem. On the other, we have the negatives of ambition and conceit.

churches, or not in church? They should have been trained, empowered, and activated into works of ministry. Why do people who were once full of fire for Christ now refer to themselves as burn-outs?

## MINISTRY TO GOD OR MAN

Ambition and conceit are two words that seem to appear together often. Conceit has a negative connotation while ambition can be either negative or positive depending upon its degree and its expression. Conceit is the extreme of self-esteem, a positive concept. Therefore, we have, on the one hand, the positive attributes of ambition and self esteem. On the other, we have the negatives of ambition and conceit. The question seems to be: "When do the positive traits cross over to the negative? "

Ambition to do God's will and to see His kingdom established is a very worthy trait. There is negative teaching that equates ambition with a lack of humility but that is not necessarily so. One can and should be ambitious for the kingdom but humble in the execution of our ambition. If ambition for ministry is directed towards ministry to the Father as a first and foremost goal, that ambition is obviously positive. (Worship is priority number one.) If our ministry towards people follows as the second greatest commandment follows the first then that too is a positive. The problem begins to surface when our ministry towards people takes priority over our ministry towards God. This is humanistic centered and leads to an elevation of our own humanity.

Satan's greatest weapon is perversion. If he can turn us away from dependency on God for any ministry ability we have, to dependency on self, then he can successfully pervert our ministry. What follows is often a clash of ambitions. When two equally motivated and strongly gifted persons with ministry ambitions meet and their first priority is not worship, their ambitions to do service will cause them to collide. While the stronger may prevail, it may not be

122

without injury to himself, his competitors and many others. The weaker may be destroyed or debilitated.

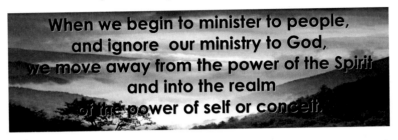

When we begin to minister to people, and ignore our ministry to God, we move away from the power of the Spirit and into the realm of the power of self or conceit.

This is one way in which people become hurt and wounded in the Body of Christ. When we begin to minister to people, and ignore our ministry to God, we move away from the power of the Spirit and into the realm of the power of self or conceit. This generally happens bit by bit until there is only the appearance of spirituality but no substance. It is at the point of departure that Jesus is no longer Lord, and Satan begins a subtle ascent, to the throne. What may have begun as an acceptable sacrifice to the Lord becomes profane as leaders become the new golden calf for the people. This means the minister becomes so high and lifted up by the people that their eyes are on the minister and not God. What he or she says becomes equal to God speaking. Then the minister has become the new golden calf. Jesus said, "My sheep know my voice." Check with the Holy Spirit and the Word of God to test every word.

How much time are we spending with God? How dependent are we for the renewal of our minds? How much of our ministry is talent without anointing and how much is gifted from God with His anointing?

## WHOSE AUTHORITY?

In order for the gifts of ministry to be exercised in the body as God has intended for them to operate, we must change our minds. You see the mind of the body cannot function for the benefit of the body unless it is aware of the needs of the body. A piece of paper does not make you a member of the body. **A member** of Christ's body is **a minister** of the body. A minister of the body must minister in the plan and authority of the body. Ministry in the body that does not follow the plan of the body will tear down rather than build up. When we minister in our own authority and our own plan, we minister out of our conceit. So all ministry is to follow the leadership that is established in the body.

Ephesians 4 tells us that when Jesus ascended he gave gifts (Doma, gift-persons) to the Church; apostles, prophets, evangelists, pastors and teachers. The purpose of these gift persons is for the perfecting of the saints for the work of ministry. That means all of us are to be prepared and activated to the work of ministry. The work of the ministry is to be done by all the saints (men and women). Jesus gave gifts. He did not give job descriptions or positions of prominence.

On the other hand someone has to be in charge. So how is this supposed to operate? The book of Acts gives us a clue. At the council of Jerusalem in the 15th chapter we see a demonstration of governance that results in a fair and equitable decision and consensus expressed by a recognized apostolic leader. The process was reevaluation, resolution and solution.

Leadership comes with gifting and character. Recognition to lead is given by those being led. So there are various arrangements for recognizing leadership in the body. On the other hand all the great leaders of the Bible were appointed by God. Sometimes they led with great difficulty as in the case of Moses. Moses led with meekness, prostrating himself before God to sway God's anger. Paul admonished and corrects often with great pleading. In many cases Biblical leaders won over the people not with force of will but by humbly pleading their case. Therefore, let us as ministers (and priests unto God) (Revelation 1:6) "**be not wise in our own conceit.**" **Rom. 12:16**

# CHAPTER THIRTEEN

## Jesus Was At Peace

### CLIMBING IN THE RUINS

The government archeologist pointed to the rock formation, "Here you see the remains of residential mikvahs." The excavated ruins at the south end of the Temple wall had been cleared, revealing many levels of civilization. Marveling at the unveiling, an untrained eye could only wonder about how the experts could discern their age. It was clear that the lovely lady knew. She had been part of the discovery team. "Those are the remains of stalls for sacrificial animals. In this place we found several coins, some Roman and some from other civilizations. There were coins with no design, only a symbol indicating their value or purpose." From this evidence, life in the time of Jesus emerges here at the foot of the Great Stairs at the south end of the Temple Mount.

According to Rabbinical law, a homeowner could not charge a visitor to the Temple for lodging. However, they could charge for taking a bath, a ritual bath or mikvah. The temple priests or the homeowners could also charge for sacrificial animals and most of all for changing the Roman or other coinage into temple money. Some of the coins found were chits or tokens given to prove that the bearer had taken a ritual bath. How else could the priest know that the person had fulfilled this requirement? Commercial coins had to be exchanged because they showed likenesses of important people. No graven image was allowed on the Mount. It is believed that only a certain number of temple coins were in circulation. The money changers had to constantly repurchase the coins from the temple priests. A tidy profit was made by all, until the priests became greedy. (See Ezekiel 22:9-12).

## CONSUMED WITH ZEAL

The priests decided to take over the profitable money changing and animal peddling. They moved it onto the Mount, into the area called Solomon's Portico. (It had nothing to do with Solomon.) They violated their own law by allowing the coins with the graven images onto the Temple Mount. They created a monopoly, controlling prices. Costs went up. The homeowner, deprived of a major part of their revenue, escalated the price of the Mikvah. **Inflationary worship!** A poor person was virtually denied the right to worship and sacrifice. The sight of the 'New Dealing' was the only place that a Gentile was allowed to be on the Temple Mount. The spectacle and confusion that resulted was certainly no great witness to the non-Jew. Gentiles came to worship God. They were only allowed in the Court of the Gentiles which now housed the money changers (franchised by the priests). The priests had forgotten that their duty was to stand between the people and God as intercessors ministering God's word and love to the people. The priests were to be a light to the gentiles.

Are you training up yourself to respond in peace or in angry warfare? The choice lies within. A person who prepares not to be offended has a better shot at peace.

Into this debacle of greed, usury, and unjust gain entered Jesus. Can you imagine the revulsion He must have felt? Greed had perverted the House of Prayer for All Nations.

Satan is always the great perverter. It follows, therefore, that Satan had gotten a foothold onto the Temple Mount. Jesus was consumed with zeal for his Father's House, a fulfillment of prophecy (Psalms 69:9). That's a nice way to say that He was angry.

## FOUNDATION

**ROMANS 12:17-18** "Recompense to no man evil for evil; Provide for things honest in the sight of all men. If it be possible, as much as lieth in you, live peaceably with all men."

## TEMPER, TEMPER

Have you ever lost your temper? Isn't that a silly way of saying it. Nobody ever loses their temper. What they lose is control. Or do they? Really what they do is to make a decision. Sometimes it's almost an instantaneous decision. Almost!

Let's be 'honest in the sight of all men.' In that split second before one acts upon his bad temper, he has a choice to make. Sometimes it seems like a spontaneous reaction. That is the result of training the mind to follow a certain pattern of behavior. That is a conscious choice.

## PEACE WITHIN

Peace is a conscious choice. Are you training up yourself to respond in peace, or in angry warfare? The choice lies within. A person who prepares not to be offended has a better shot at peace. If you say to yourself, "I will not be offended. I choose to be at peace. I choose to take no offense." Then you probably won't. Instead of reacting to an offensive situation, you will be prepared for peace, real inner peace.

## A PLACE FOR ANGER

Does that mean as a Christian I must never get angry? No, that would be phony and it wouldn't follow Christ's example. Scripture says, "Be angry and sin not" **(Eph 4:26)**. Anger is not sin. It's what you do with your anger that may result in sin. If anger moves you to vengeance, that's sin. Revenge is sin. "Vengeance is mine, I will repay, saith the Lord." Recompensing evil with evil is sin.

So what do I do with my anger? Do I swallow it up inside? Definitely not! Your anger must be dealt with. Let's look at some different kinds of anger and see how they can be dealt with so that no sin will be involved.

## ZEAL FOR GOD

Our zeal for God demands that we get angry about the desecration of holy things. Make sure that it's a holy thing that you're angry about, however, not some pet peeve. Jesus made a decision to show His displeasure. I don't believe that He lost control in the process. The braiding of the cords shows a very deliberate act. Jesus' purpose was to restore the state of holiness to the Temple. It is interesting that no one tried to stop Him. No one condemned Him or tried to arrest Him. They knew that what was happening was wrong. When Jesus had completed the cleansing of the Temple, He went on with His plan for the day. He did not dwell on the offense. Jesus was at peace. He did not chase after the people and continue to press His cause. He knew what His purpose was and He returned to what He had intended to do in the first place.

So the first test for the righteous venting of zealous anger is that it must be motivated by desire to bring restoration of the holy. Secondly, our act should be deliberate. The consequences should be well thought out. Whether the act is physical, verbal, or written, we must remain in control and be at peace. And remember, Jesus was without sin and He constantly renewed His mind. So it would be a good idea to talk over your decision with a person of Godly wisdom.

## OFFENSES WILL COME

To walk with the Lord is to be at odds with the world. At some point confrontations will occur. People will misunderstand us, distort the truth, and lie about us. These things will anger and hurt us. Often the hurts come through Christians who themselves have been hurt. Many times poor communication or reception may be at fault.

Matthew 18 lays out a three step process to follow in such a case. The only problem with the steps is that <u>too few people ever really follow them through.</u>

First, let's determine if the offense is worthy of our anger. A simple communication may set the record straight. On the other hand, we may determine that the act was purposeful and coming from malicious intent. **Matthew 18** lays out a three step process to follow in such a case. The only problem with the steps is that too few people ever really follow them through. We tend to get involved in the 'what ifs' rather than simply trusting God and doing His directions even when the walk becomes a marathon. If we do as He tells us the outcome will be His problem. Don't you think it's always better to trust God and leave the results up to Him? We don't really have any control over outcomes anyhow.

## TWO RESPONSES

There are really only two responses to anger. However you disguise it, revenge is the usual motive. But we have already ruled out revenge as belonging only to God. <u>Revenge in man is sin</u>. So what's left?

Let's think of Jesus on the cross. How do you think He felt when the nails were driven into His hands? Aside from the anguish of pain what was His predominant emotion. I think it had to be anger. Jesus was a total man and He experienced all the emotions of any natural man. If somebody hurts me, I get mad. So do you. So does everybody.

What did Jesus do with the anger He felt? He forgave. You see, that's the key. "Be angry and sin not." What was happening was wrong to His sinless person. To cry out in condemnation would have been a greater wrong. ("God **made** him who had no **sin** to be **sin** for us.") 2 Cor. 5:21 NIV Sin had no defense .By His supreme sacrifice Jesus showed us the right release. "**Father, forgive them**...." (Luke22:34) **Restoration** ("...and the God of Peace will crush Satan under your feet." (**Romans 16:20**)

So the second reaction to anger, and the only allowable one for a Christian, is forgiveness. <u>Forgiveness brings peace</u>. "As much as lieth within you...."

## FOUNDATIONS

**John 14:27** "Peace I leave with you, my <u>peace</u> I give unto you; not as the world giveth, give I you. Let not your heart be troubled, neither let it be afraid."

**Isaiah 9:7** "Of the increase of His government and <u>peace</u> there shall be no end."

 **26:3** "Thou shalt keep him in perfect <u>peace</u> whose mind is stayed on thee."

 **93:4** "The chastisement of our <u>peace</u> was upon him."

 **54:10** ...Covenant of <u>peace</u> shall not be removed."

## COVENANT OF PEACE

The sacrifice of peace was without blemish. If you belong to Jesus then He has given perfect peace.

The KEY is within.
The Kingdom of God is within.
The Kingdom of God is righteousness, peace and joy.
The work of righteousness is peace.
The product of peace is joy.
The KEY is in the heart.

What troubles your heart? Give it to Jesus. Take this advice. It's powerful. What ever troubles you, pray: "JESUS TAKE THIS!" Keep praying. Don't stop until it's gone. A week, a month, a year, keep it up. Quietly, imperceptibly, suddenly it's gone! GLORY! Jesus took it.

**What causes you to anger?**
Consider the lilies.
Jesus was at PEACE.

He purchased it, and then He gave it to us.

# CHAPTER FOURTEEN

# Envy and Rebellion or Trust and Do Good

## A CLOUD OF SMOKE AND A HEARTY HI—HO FLIVVER

Flivver: SLANG, a cheap or dilapidated old car.
Webster's Dictionary of the English Language, Modern Promotions, (1982), Canada.

Although I didn't often put it to the test, I knew that I could run over or away from almost anything on the road. I enjoyed my '78 Ford pickup with the patchwork paint. It wasn't classy. My wife prayed daily for a more suitable car. This then fifty year old pastor, perpetually in need of a diet, liked to hunt and fish as much as he liked to preach. So for me, the venerable hauler's utility outweighed its liabilities.

One particular morning I was driving leisurely. From my comfortably slouched position, I was jarred upright by a streak of blazing red that appeared immediately before my front bumper. Instinctively, my right leg stiffened as it slammed the accelerator. My old behemoth bolted upright in pursuit of the smaller vehicle. Then it was gone. I never caught the sleek Porsche 911 that would have been the dream of my youth and an old man's fancy. But I got close enough to read the license plate: '4U2ENVY.' It took but a second to get the message: **For you to envy**. That's just not fair, is it?

## FOUNDATIONS

**Romans 12:19-20**: "Dearly beloved, avenge not yourselves, but rather give place unto wrath: for it is written, Vengeance is mine; I will repay, saith the Lord. Therefore if thine enemy hunger, feed him; if he thirst, give him drink: for in so doing thou shalt heap coals of fire on his head."

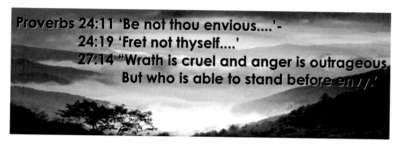

Proverbs 24:11 'Be not thou envious....'-
24:19 'Fret not thyself....'
27:14 "Wrath is cruel and anger is outrageous,
But who is able to stand before envy.'

**Psalm 37:1-2** "Fret not thyself because of evildoers, neither be thou envious against the workers of iniquity."

verse **7** "...fret not thyself..."
verse **8** "...fret not thyself...."

## POINTING THE FINGER

There is nothing to envy in position. The higher the position, the higher the responsibility and the heavier the burden is.

Through that license plate, the Lord opened my eyes. There was some envy in my life. I don't need envy and neither do you. A great deal of our fretting is birthed by envy. Envy of success, position, or situation leads to fretting. God doesn't want to hear it. He stops His ears to murmurings. Jude reports on 'certain men' (vs.4) who 'perished in the gainsaying of Cor-e,' who were murmerers, complainers...,' Cor-e and Korah of the Old Testament are the same person. Psalm 106 tells us that they rebelled because they were envious.

# KORAH'S REBELLION

The story of Korah in Numbers 16 shows us that they were people of limited spiritual insight. Let's examine Korah's complaints. First, they came against the position of Aaron and Moses. They said everybody was holy; thus no one should be lifted up above anyone else. They mistook Godly appointed and anointed authority for self elevation. God had placed his authority to govern His people in Moses. There is nothing to envy in position. The higher the position; the higher the responsibility, the heavier the burden is. When hurts come they hurt more intensely. When mistakes and errors are made, the authority is held in greater accountability. So don't strive for position.

What did Moses do when they challenged his person? He fell on his face before the Lord on their behalf. When they challenged his godly authority, he got angry. Moses was the meekest man on earth. What was the difference? They said, "It's a small thing (is it?) that thou hast brought us up out of the land that flowed with milk and honey to kill us in the wilderness; except thou makest thyself a prince over us." That's the challenge to authority. "You made yourself a prince." How inaccurate! Moses wasn't anxious for the job. As a matter of fact, he tried to give it away. He said, "I can't talk. Who am I to go out and represent the Lord?"

The Lord replied, "Okay, I'll fix that for you. I'll give you a mouthpiece, but you're not getting out of the job." (RRV= Robert's Revised Version) When the mantle falls, the mantle falls. You can get a ship for Tarshis, you won't get away from the mantle. If by chance you are so stubborn that you won't submit, God will use someone else. Oh, the price you will pay.

Why did they challenge his authority? The envy factor was at work. Their eyes were on only the immediate and obvious. They looked backward instead of forward. They thought: "We had enough to eat; we had a roof over our heads; we didn't depend on having quail fly into our hands;

we didn't go out and pick up our manna, whatever it was. We could have the things we were used to having." They got their eyes on their present difficulties and forgot how it really was back in Egypt. They said to Moses, "What! Are you going to put out the eyes of the people?" Moses fell before the Lord and the Lord spoke to him. "We will take care of it tomorrow, not today, tomorrow."(RRV) (Remember God's wrath never falls until all chance of repentance is gone.) He gave them the night to think it over. Then he said, "This is what you do: Take your censers and fill them with incense. Set them on fire. Say, 'We will see who the Lord chooses." So on the 'morrow they did exactly that.

Now Korah's people had already set up their own worship place. Their rebellion had been sealed. When Moses bid them to come down they refused. "We will not come; we will not submit to you; we have made up our own minds." So God said to Moses, "Get Out of the way. I'll strike them dead."

Moses protested, "Wait a minute, God. For the sin of the one will you kill them all?" (Paraphrase) "Alright, Moses," The Lord responded. Moses really could take it to God. (So can you) "You tell the others to get away and I will not destroy them." (Paraphrase)

Moses went down and told the people to get away. Many did, but some did not. Korah and his henchmen came out of the tent. This is one of those instances in the Bible that we don't like. There were women and little children involved. Destruction of the rebellious men we can handle. Slaughter of the 'innocents,' however, ruffles our humanity. These were the non-combatants, so-to-speak. Was justice served by their deaths? Don't get your humanity confused with God's holiness and justice. He knows best. When a man rebels he enters into a curse, he curses his family and all who are close to him. They, however innocent, begin to operate in that curse. (ALL SIN HAS CORPORATE CONSEQUENCE) God knew that the curse had to be stopped before it spread.

Fire fell. The earth opened. They were swallowed up---everybody! Could God have done it in a different way? If there was any other way God would have done it. His mercy always goes before His judgment.

## THE REBEL IS DEAD, BUT LONG LIVE THE REBEL

Moses had said that if something natural happened then I am not a man of God. If something supernatural happened, however, then the people remaining would know that it was God. Somehow, the 250 censers of incense did not get swallowed up. Even though these people were in rebellion to God, through His delegated authority, the censers were preserved. You see, they had been dedicated to God. The people perished but the evidence of their ministry remained. Moses commanded that the censers be gathered and hammered out to make a covering for the altar. They were dedicated to God. They were holy. They could not be destroyed. Is it possible that a thing dedicated to God in rebellion remains holy? The thing was holy, but what happened to the rebels?

> Don't get your humanity confused with God's holiness and justice. He knows best.

You think that would be the end of the story and the rest of the people would come into line. No! On the next day the remainder rose up and said to Moses, "It was all your fault." The Bible tells us, "Rebellion is as the sin of witchcraft" (1 Sam. 15:23). Witchcraft clouds the minds. Witchcraft flows over the people and sets a curse in operation. Witchcraft flies around and spreads confusion. When you pervert the things of God, you spread confusion.

As an example, men don't sleep with men, women don't sleep with women, and human beings don't have sex with

137

animals because that is confusion. God said, "...Let the land produce living creatures after their own kind." (Gen 1:24) It would be confusion of the five—fold purpose of creation. (See Genesis 1:28-Be fruitful, 2)Multiply, 3) Replenish, 4) Subdue, 5) Have dominion.) Acting out of the order of God, away from the authority of God, always brings confusion.

The whole congregation rose up against Moses and said, "You killed those people. Are you going to kill us too?" God said, "Get out of the way, Moses." He began to strike them with a plague. Moses ordered Aaron, "Get the censers. Get out there between God and the people and stay the plague." Aaron stood between the living and the dead and lifted the censer. That is the job of the priest, to intercede for the people, even risking his own life if need be, **to stay the judgment of God**. The plague was stopped. (Ezekiel 22:30 "...and I looked for a man to stand before me in the GAP for the land that I might not destroy it. But I found no one...")

## GOD HAS A ROOT.

Again, you would think that the people had seen enough. The rebel was dead but now the people had taken the rebel's part. It all stemmed from the root of envy. God has another root. God said, "Tell every one of those leaders out there to give me their staff. Gather them all together and put Aaron's staff in the middle."

Aaron's staff was very special. It looked like a dead stick. Pharaoh thought so, but when Aaron's rod hit the ground it became a live snake. The magicians said, "We can do that too." When they did it, their sticks became snakes also. However, Aaron's snake then swallowed up the magicians' snakes. Aaron picked it up and it became a rod again; a supernatural rod.

Rabbinical legend (from The Jewish Encyclopedia) tells us about that staff. Jethro, Moses' father-in-law, was in the court of Pharaoh as the Priest of Midian. When Joseph's possessions were being divided up, the rod came to Jethro.

Jethro returned to Midian and stuck the rod in the ground. No one could remove it; it was stuck tight. Moses came to Midian and saw the rod. By the inscriptions on it, he recognized that it was Abraham's rod. This rod had been handed down from Abraham to Isaac to Jacob to Joseph. Moses pulled the rod from the ground. This showed that he was the heir to leadership. Sound familiar? The same story is repeated in mythology, folk—tales and religions, but the Moses story is the oldest. Moses gave the rod to Aaron. Now, as the legend goes, Aaron gave the rod to Moses to be put with the others. (Number 17:4)

Aaron's rod looked like a dead stick. So did all the others. (A lot of times the things of God may look like they're dead.) They put all those rods into the Tabernacle. The next morning you know what happened? Aaron's rod not only had buds, but it had leaves, flowers, and almonds! It bore fruit overnight. The thing that looks like a dead stick, God can cause to bud, and it will bear fruit overnight.

Our eyes may tell us that it's a dead stick. We see no way out. We may say we can't make it because we're too few. There's not enough money or perhaps not enough people. But if we would just put it in the Tabernacle it will bear fruit! It'll grow beyond our imagination. It is the Lord God who justifies, and it is He who gives the increase. (I Cor 3:7) Your hopes, your dreams, your prophetic word may seem dead. There is no way they can come to pass. Let's put them in the tabernacle of God's presence and see what happens. I did that to my "Isaac" (our ministry) which was on the sacrificial altar and looked dead. Thirty years later God raised it up suddenly in one day.

## OUT OF THE PIT

It was envy that caused Joseph to be cast into the pit. It was envy that caused Daniel to be cast into the pit. Joseph and Daniel are two of the 'white knights' of the Bible. They did nothing wrong. They did only good.

139

Eventually, they got out of their pits. Then they were more powerful than before. **The only way to overcome envy is with good.** Even the stored-up good done from the past is able to return and to overcome the evil of the present. Are you in some kind of pit today? Then do good. Do good to those who are your enemies, to those who persecute you, and envy you. Psalm thirty-seven says to "Fret not...Trust in the Lord... Do good... and you shall possess the land." That dead stick will bloom and the land you possess will flow with milk and honey.

## FINDING MILK AND HONEY

Getting the milk and honey out of the land takes some sweat. I have never seen a more fertile land than Israel. The orange, grapefruit, and banana groves are fantastic even more productive than the ones I have seen in Florida and California. The fields in Israel have borders of huge rocks which have been pushed to either side. For nearly 2000 years nothing but rocks covered much of the land. People thought the land was barren. One man was inspired to get a bulldozer and push the rocks out of the way. The soil wasn't even rocky underneath. Underneath those rocks there was extremely fertile soil waiting while the land had its Sabbaths of rest. The topsoil should have been gone but it was not.

When the Turks cut down the trees in Israel, they utterly raped the land of timber. Israel was a barren place. When the trees are gone, the topsoil washes away, but in Israel it didn't. When God says that a place will flow with milk and honey, nothing can change it.

Trust in the Lord and do good and you will possess the land. (Psalm 37:3) Even if the land looks barren when you get it, trust Him. Even if the land looks full of rocks when you get it, trust Him. Bend your back a little and push the rocks out of the way. Don't be envious of that guy over there with the fertile looking hill. If God gives it to you, your topsoil will make his green look brown. Push the rocks out of the way. Underneath you will find more fertile dirt than you ever imagined. It's time to get your bulldozer moving. Start pushing rocks out of the way. Trust in God because He has ordered it for thousands of years. He did not take you out in the wilderness for you to perish. Trust in the Lord, do good, and possess the land. Don't you think it's time you possessed the land? Don't you think its time you got your bulldozer rolling? Don't you think its time to put "4U2ENVY" to bed? There is no reason for you to have envy in your life.

## SAY IT.

### _Say this out loud:_

1) I will not fret.
2) I will not be envious.
3) I will trust in the Lord.
4) I will do good.
5) I will possess the Land.

# CHAPTER FIFTEEN

## Overcoming Or Being Overcome

### THREE BLOCKADES: FEAR, GREED, UNBELIEF.

FEAR is the opposite of faith. Dr. Edwin Lewis Cole said that Fear is the belief that what hasn't happened will happen. He also said that Faith is the belief that what hasn't happened will happen. That's right, they're the same. It takes just as much energy and belief to have Fear as to have Faith. Faith is positive. Fear is negative. Faith is progressive. Fear is regressive. Faith rewards. Fear penalizes. Faith activates. Fear paralyzes. Faith is pleasing to God. Fear is failure to believe in God and His Word. "Without faith it is impossible to please God." **Hebrews 11:6**

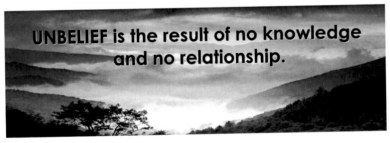

UNBELIEF is the result of no knowledge and no relationship.

GREED says that there is never enough. Greed is the belief that if you hang onto everything, you can just keep adding to it.

UNBELIEF is the result of no knowledge and no relationship. Unbelief means that I cannot trust, therefore, I must do it myself.

# BLOCKADED

When I am operating in the <u>Three Blockades,</u> I suffer a lack of power. Three areas of my life that are always affected are <u>finances, health, and relationships</u>.

**FINANCES**: Fear holds back my prosperity. Boldness is required in any case to obtain a financial blessing. Operating with no debt, giving liberally, and managing wisely is living according to God's Word and trusting Him. The person who fails to follow with trust finds himself in debt and unmanageable turmoil. He fails to see that the cost of his failure to give abundantly is greater than the amount given. The successful Christian realizes that 100% of what he has is God's. The small portion (at least 10%) is not a sacrifice but the portion left is the blessing.

**HEALTH:** Fear causes stress. STRESS IS A MAJOR CAUSE OF MOST MALADIES. Worry is a form of stress. Greed causes worry over possessions. Unbelief keeps one from accepting the healing.

**RELATIONSHIPS**: Fear will bring about a loss of friendships. Greed leads to damaging actions through a desire to be popular. Unbelief keeps us from giving the best of ourselves to those we call our friends. The best that we have is the **Word of God**.

> **Unbelief keeps us from giving the best of ourselves to those we call our friends.**

**When we fail to witness to unsaved friends, we rob them and ourselves**. When we fail to confront ungodly behavior, we put both ourselves and our friends in jeopardy. This failure to trust God's Word as never returning void, is really a sign of our unbelief.

# FOUNDATIONS:

**Rom.12:21** "Be not overcome of evil, but overcome evil with good."

  **14:23** "...whatsoever is not of faith is sin."

  **15:19** "...I would have you wise unto that which is good and simple concerning evil."

## GOOD OVERCOMES EVIL

When the Pharisee referred to Jesus as "Good Master...." He replied, "Why do you call me good? Only God is good." From this we can deduce that good is that which contains or represents God. Good is the presence of godliness.

Satan is the essence of all that is evil. Satan is opposed to all that is godly. We could say, therefore, that evil is the absence of godliness.

To overcome is to take by force or to convert. **Matthew 11:12** says, "From the days of John the Baptist until now the kingdom of heaven has suffered violence, and men of violence take it by force." In another translation violence is translated as force or forceful. It is time to be violent (forceful) about godliness. Why did he say from the time of John the Baptist? What did John do that caused violence in the Kingdom? First of all John broke with tradition. He was the son of a priest and it would have been expected that he follow in his father's footsteps to become a Levitical priest. He didn't. Instead he went off into the wilderness to preach and baptize; to prepare The Way of the Lord. He prepared the way for a new priesthood **(the priesthood of the order of Melchezidek)** <u>to be established for a new covenant.</u> Secondly he preached repentance. When one repents, one takes away the ground that the enemy has stolen from you and you redeem your land. You bring the principles of the Kingdom to bear on the situation. Satan's Kingdom is defeated and Christ's Kingdom is expanded.

Let's show forth with power that God is able, through His people, to overcome. Social programs and entitlements do not correct social ills. Social programs may alleviate the effects of the situation but there is rarely any lasting effect. Indeed such programs may actually compound the problem. People may become passively dependent on the programs and develop an entitlement mentality. Social action does not cause lives to change. **Only the gospel strongly spoken will cause people to repent (change).** God's people never have been a force for social change except by the preaching of the gospel. The reason is simple. When men are converted, they exchange the absence of godliness for the presence of godliness. **Evil is overcome by good.**

When men are converted, they exchange the absence of godliness for the presence of godliness. **Evil is overcome by good.**

## CHOICES

What choices have you made that have kept you from overcoming? That's right, I said, "...choices...."

There are really only two choices:
1) To be overcome by evil.
2) To overcome by the presence of godliness.

Does that sound familiar? It should. Remember, in **Romans 12:2**, we discussed being conformed to the world or being transformed. In **Romans 12:3**, we found that transformation comes by grace given to us. The things of God always boil down to choices and it's usually a case of either/or.

Blessing or Curse
Transformed or Conformed
Saved or Lost
Obedience or Rebellion
Forgiven or Condemned
Overcome or Be Overcome

In each case God initiates and God fulfills. The choice is to come into agreement with what the covenant offers and receive the blessing or to refuse to agree and suffer the curse. God does not pull our strings. He lets us make our choices. When we come into agreement with His terms, the fulfillment is up to Him. In this way we initiate or create with God's power.

## HOW TO BE AN OVERCOMER

1. **Worship** - Present yourself as a living sacrifice. Do it daily, regularly, consistently, publically and privately, formally and informally. Make worship priority one. Pray without ceasing.

2. **Study** - Read God's Word every day. Read whole chapters and study whole books at a time. Get study helps. Take formal classes. Take notes during sermons and teachings. Review your notes.

3. **Self Evaluate** - Take note of what you are doing. Examine your attitudes. Look at Jesus as the only standard. When you fail, ask forgiveness and pray for power.

4. **Unify the Body** - The Body of Christ that is the local Bible believing church, home group or other assembly in your area, is the most powerful unit of people on the earth. Work for unity in your church and in the church at large. Remember that body unity only comes when there is body authority that is governed by the nature of Christ.

5. **Demonstrate your Giftedness** - Develop and pray for spiritual gifts. Utilize your gifts for the purpose of

ministry. Remember that all ministries begin with ministry to the Father.

6. **Be Christ like** - Be a Christian in your behavior. Remember that you represent the Lord in all that you are and do. When people see you, they should see Jesus.

7. **Give no place for wrath** - Be prepared to live at peace. Don't let your peace become conditional on the behavior of others. Determine now not to take offense.

8. **Overcome** - Bring the presence of godliness into every situation.

9. **Develop** a godly character and godly responses.

*Choose* victory! *Choose* blessing! *Choose* obedience! *Choose* to overcome!

## FIVE FOLD PURPOSE.

God's five fold purpose of creation is stated in Genesis 1:28:

> 1 - Be fruitful.
> 2 - Multiply.
> 3 - Replenish.
> 4 - Subdue.
> 5 - Have dominion.

If every one of your motives is tempered by God's purpose for you in creation, you will be always fulfilling His purpose. The transforming of your mind places you in the position of being in God's good and perfect and acceptable will.

## ROBERT'S RAZOR

"Rules without relationship will be broken; relationship without rules cannot last."

## CHOOSE TO OVERCOME

Say the following affirmations out loud:
**TODAY I REJECT DEFEAT!**
**TODAY I CHOOSE VICTORY!**
**TODAY I CHOOSE TO OVERCOME!**

*Robert blowing shofar at entrance to dock leading to St. Clements Island, Maryland, site of Lord Baltimore's first landing.*

# EPILOGUE

# A Needle In The Hand Of God

## Isaac    O.T.A.

"You know what we have to do, don't you?" "Yes, we have to put **Isaac on the altar**." Annette and I were sitting in the car facing each other in the dark. We had just left a prayer meeting where God had spoken to each of us separately. There was no argument. We knew what we had to do.

"Isaac" was the Christian school ministry we had founded nearly five years earlier. Putting "Isaac on the altar" meant that we were going to lay down our claims and walk away. We would be leaving behind a thriving ministry that we had built by personal sacrifice. We had worked for five years of seventy and eighty hour weeks; thousands of dollars of personal funds and lost income had been invested. For the first time in several weeks, we were able to settle down to a quiet sleep that night. We knew that God was in charge and that there was nothing for us to do but surrender.

WAS THIS THE WAY IT WAS TO END? Were our dreams and sacrifices to be all gone? Were we failures, forced to leave a thriving but always struggling ministry? Had we been foolish dreamers when five years before we had left promising careers to pursue a vision with such joy and expectation? What would we do now? All of our professional bridges had been burned behind us.

Now God had spoken to us "Put Isaac on the Altar." That was that.

The first week we did very little. I sat and stared; the tears wouldn't even come. Annette cried. I tried to comfort her, but I couldn't do it very well. We read the Bible, not even looking for answers. On Sunday we went to a faraway church and became anonymously lost in a sea of unfamiliar faces. The next week I fussed at God. Why had I prayed my way through only to have this result? Why had I felt so certain of God's leading? What had gone wrong? NO ANSWERS!

## GOD'S CAUSE

I was in the basement working when a Scripture came to my mind. I picked up the Bible which I had been reading and turned to the story of Samson. From Judges 13:1, I read through the story but I stopped cold at chapter fourteen, verse four. The American Version translated by J.M.P. Smith says it this way: "...**it was at the instigation of the Lord that he was picking a quarrel....**" The King James says that, "God needed a cause...." Please don't misinterpret what I thought I understood. This has no reference to any other party. God simply made me aware that by surrendering all my life to Him I became His instrument for His purpose. God was doing something and I didn't need to know the details.

At first I was stunned and then a little angry. As I realized the immensity of what He was showing me I began to feel a little foolish and humble. God had needed me to accomplish His purpose. He showed me that I had indeed heard from Him. The situation I had initiated and the outcome of my actions were not the end of the matter. It was simply the cause which God had initiated for His purpose.

## LIKE A NEEDLE PULLING THREAD

Think of a sewing needle. The sharp point penetrates the material, the eye accommodates the thread. In the hand of a skilled seamstress a tear is mended or two fabrics are joined. God is skilled at mending and joining. Are you willing to be His needle? Wait before you answer. You see, it's not as simple as it looks.

As a needle is inserted into a cloth the needle point is ever so slightly dulled. Hundreds of stitches later the needle may be so worn that it is no longer usable. Sharp needles are used on natural fiber and woven materials. On 'miracle fibers,' such as polyester and knits, a ball point needle is used. The difference is that a sharp needle makes a hole by piercing the material. A ball point needle separates the threads in the knit, allowing the needle to pass through without breaking any of the material's fibers. The eye of the needle is also subject to minute wear. As the thread is pulled through by the needle, the tension wears on the eye. The eye gradually becomes elongated and enlarged.

Are you willing to be used as a needle in the hand of God? God needs instruments to carry His love and correction. He repairs the rents and joins the fabrics of our lives. Different instruments are suited to different situations. The instrument is subject to wear. Under the skillful hand of God the sharp instrument may become blunted and the narrow eye may become enlarged only to be refitted by the Master to a new purpose. Are you ready?

## POWERFUL PRAYERS

I believe that the following are the most powerful prayers we can give to God.

1) **The prayer of repentance.**
This prayer ushers in change.
2) **The prayer for the infilling of the Holy Spirit.**
This prayer takes us out of the natural into the supernatural.
3) **The prayer for commission or ministry.**
"Jesus, tell me what to do, and whatever it is I'll do it."
4) **The prayer for wisdom.**
So that we can live according to His plan.
5) **The prayer of consecration.**
So that He gets all the credit.

If you are ready now to be a needle in the hand of God, sit down and write out each of these five prayers.

Don't be satisfied until they express your heart precisely.

Communicate them to your helpmate. Then start praying and don't stop, ever.

## REFITTED BY THE MASTER

My point had been blunted and my eye had been elongated just like the long used needle. I asked the air the simple question: "What am I going to do with the rest of my life and dreams?" The air didn't have any answers. It seemed like God didn't either.

I put together a resume and started to look for employment. I had plenty of qualifications; the problem was that they just didn't come together in the business world. I received answers like, 'Over qualified', 'No recent experience in the field', or 'Stale technologically'. I had some great interviews. Employers seemed interested until they asked me about my ministry work. Their major fear was that I would work for them only a short time and then go back to ministry.

I had several job offers, but I knew that they weren't right for me. Annette and I looked at several businesses to buy. Somehow each one seemed a poor investment of our funds and skills.

Fortunately, Annette had just received an inheritance that kept us afloat. There were also gifts from saints who still supported us. A small group formed in our home for prayer and Bible study. We began to understand that nothing had changed in God's eyes. He had called us to a work of ministry and He hadn't changed His mind. When God puts a call on your life to do a work of ministry, the call remains until He changes or rescinds it. The circumstances that were surrounding our lives were just that, circumstances. We had succumbed to the circumstances but God had not. We understood that we were to go forward with the ministry to which he had called us.

Instead of reacting to the circumstances we began to initiate. We formed a new ministry. This time we established a church first, then a school. Like Isaac in Genesis, we were digging a new well. We were able to purchase a former public school building. Everything was done in prayer. On the last Sunday in June, less than six months had passed since we had put 'Isaac on the altar', we held our first service in the new building. Our Christian school opened that following September. It was a new beginning with an enlarged vision.

That's not the end of the story. There is much more to be said. There are new works and new revelations. The journey for us has just begun. Little did we know that **thirty years** after putting Isaac on the Altar, we would hear God speak at the lunch table to check on the legal status of the ministry we had laid on the altar. The State Taxation department told us the corporation was still viable and all we had to do was to start using it. **Isaac was alive!** After thirty years our Revelation 22 ministry was resurrected! Even the federal tax status was still intact.

The ministry, once again awakened, moves forward toward reformation in the church, revival of its people, and transformation of the earth.

*Barbara and Randy Walter praying "on site with insight"
at the Baltimore Harbor*